Vírago
AWAKENING A WARRIOR

PATRICE E. HUGHLEY

DIVINE WORKS PUBLISHING, LLC.
Royal Palm Beach, Florida

© 2024 Patrice E. Hughley

All Rights Reserved. No part of this publication may be reproduced, stored in a retrieval system, or transmitted in any form or by any means, electronic, mechanical, photocopying, recording or otherwise without the prior permission of the publisher or in accordance with the provisions of the Copyright, Designs, and Patents Act 1988 or under the terms of any license permitting limited copying issued by the Copyright Licensing Agency.

The views expressed in this work are solely those of the author and do not necessarily reflect the views of the publisher, the publisher hereby disclaims any responsibility for them.

Except where noted, all scriptures included were taken from the King James Bible, and used with permission. 1. New International Version (NIV)** – Scripture quotations taken from *The Holy Bible, New International Version® (NIV)*. Copyright © 1973, 1978, 1984, 2011 by Biblica, Inc. Used by permission. All rights reserved worldwide. 2. New King James Version (NKJV)** – Scripture quotations taken from *The New King James Version*. Copyright © 1982 by Thomas Nelson. Used by permission. All rights reserved.* 3. Amplified Bible (AMP)** – Scripture quotations taken from *The Amplified® Bible*. Copyright © 2015 by The Lockman Foundation. Used by permission. www.Lockman.org. 4. English Standard Version (ESV)** – Scripture quotations taken from *The Holy Bible, English Standard Version® (ESV)*. Copyright © 2001 by Crossway, a publishing ministry of Good News Publishers. Used by permission. All rights reserved. 5. Complete Jewish Bible (CJB)** – Scripture quotations taken from *The Complete Jewish Bible* by David H. Stern. Copyright © 1998 by Jewish New Testament Publications, Inc. Used by permission. All rights reserved. 6. The Message (MSG)** – Scripture quotations taken from *The Message*. Copyright © 1993, 2002, 2018 by Eugene H. Peterson. Used by permission of NavPress. All rights reserved. Represented by Tyndale House Publishers, Inc. 7. New Living Translation (NLT)** – Scripture quotations taken from *The Holy Bible, New Living Translation (NLT)*. Copyright © 1996, 2004, 2007, 2013 by Tyndale House Foundation. Used by permission of Tyndale House Publishers, Inc., Carol Stream, Illinois 60188. All rights reserved. 8. Common English Bible (CEB)** – Scripture quotations taken from *The Common English Bible (CEB)*. Copyright © 2011 by Common English Bible. Used by permission. All rights reserved. 9. New Revised Standard Version (NRSV)** – Scripture quotations taken from *The New Revised Standard Version Bible (NRSV)*, copyright © 1989 by the Division of Christian Education of the National Council of the Churches of Christ in the USA. Used by permission. All rights reserved.

Library of Congress Control Number (LCCN): 2024942677

ISBN-13: 978-1-949105-76-6 (hardback)

ISBN-13: 978-1-949105-67-4 (paperback)

ISBN-13: 978-1-949105-67-4 (eBook)

First Edition Published: 12/14/2024

Printed in the United States of America

www.DivineWorksPublishing.com
561-990-BOOK (2665)

The Lord is close to the brokenhearted

and saves those who are crushed in spirit.

—Psalm 34:18

(New International Version)

DEDICATION

This book is dedicated to the brokenhearted.

To those who feel rejected, forgotten, or alone.

To those in pain and grieving.

To those that have lost their way, or themselves, in the chaos—this is for you.

As I escort you through this "tragedy to triumph story," I'll explain how to get out of that pit, so that you can be whole and live again.

I pray the Love and Grace of Almighty God give you beauty for ashes, the oil of joy for mourning, and the garment of praise for the spirit of heaviness.

(Isaiah 61:3 KJV)

This photograph was taken by Ian Spackman.
(https://commons.wikimedia.org/wiki/File:Francesco_Porzio,_Monumento_alla_difesa_di_Casale,_Piazza_Castello,_Casale_Monferrato_(Ian_Spackman_199xC_n25).jpg)

VIRAGO

Today the word ***"warrior"*** is frequently used in a broad sense to describe a person who is physically and/or mentally strong - one having great stamina in a struggle. Initially, though, it derived from an Old North French word, "werreier," meaning soldier. It first appeared in English in the 14th century, and referred to a highly skilled man of valor, one that specialized in the art of combat. Women then, were considered second class and inferior to men, mostly occupying social roles like wife, mother, or nun. However, an exceptional woman, one that exemplified characteristics and qualities of a (male) warrior, with valor and heroism, *and* while surpassing all physical expectations believed possible for her gender, was known as a ***"virago," (vi-RAH-go) [or VEE- rah- go]***.

This is the story of a traumatic season in my life meant to destroy me. But God's Grace and Mercy covered me, showing me who He is, and who I am as well.

In the Bible, the word ***virago*** appears in Genesis 2:23, when Adam names Eve:

Genesis 2:23: *"And Adam said, 'This is now bone of my bones, and flesh of my flesh; she shall be called woman, because she was taken out of man'"*

1. Old English–

A name given to Eve by Adam in Genesis 2:23 (see quot. a1425).

The name puns on the Latin word vir man and is an attempt to render a similar pun in the Hebrew word hissa.

* OE

Beo hire nama uirago, þæt is fæmne for ðan ðe heo is of hire were genumen.

Ælfric, Catholic Homilies: 1st Series (Cambridge MS. Gg.3.28) i. 182

* a1425 (c1395)

And Adam seide..this schal be clepid virago [E.V. a1425 Corpus Christi Oxford MS. 4 mannus dede; Latin virago], for she is takun of man.

Bible (Wycliffite, later version) (Royal MS.) (1850) Genesis ii. 23

* 1547

First whan a woman was made of god she was named Virago because she dyd come of a man.

A. Borde, Breuiary of Helthe i. f. lxxxxiiii

* 1576

Before Eua sinned, she was called Virago, and after she sinned she deserued to be called Eua.

G. Gascoigne, translation of Pope Innocent III, 1st Bk. Vewe Worldly Vanities in Droomme of Doom

* 1591 (?a1425)

Fleshe of my fleshe shee hase..Therfore shee shalbe called, iwisse, 'viragoo'.

Adam & Eve (Huntington MS.) in R. M. Lumiansky & D. Mill, Chester Mystery Cycle (1974) vol. I. 19 (Middle English Dictionary)

* 1865

God sends him to sleep, and then creates Eve from one of his ribs; and Adam welcomes her by the name 'Virago'.

Journal Royal Inst. Cornwall April 6

* 1938

The virago in question is Eve, who has just been created.

Modern Language Notes vol. 53 33

* 2009

Adam, because she had been formed from his bones and flesh, called her virago, woman, taken from vir, man.

https://www.oed.com/dictionary/virago_n?tl=true

Vírago
AWAKENING A WARRIOR

PREFACE XIII
INTRODUCTION XV
CHPT 1 THE SETUP... 1
CHPT 2 THE ASSIGNMENT... 11
CHPT 3 THE ENCOUNTER... 17
CHPT 4 THE BREACH... 25
CHPT 5 THE FIRST FIGHT... 35
CHPT 6 A NEW JOURNEY BEGINS... 43
CHPT 7 RETURN TO BASE... 47
CHPT 8 A RISING STORM... 51
CHPT 9 A SURPRISE ATTACK... 57
CHPT 10 CONFRONTING CONFUSION... 63
CHPT 11 CONFLICTED... 77
CHPT 12 BEHIND ENEMY LINES... 85
CHPT 13 GOD IN THE MIDST... 99
CHPT 14 PIVOT... 115
CHPT 15 THE RECKONING... 119
CHPT 16 THE PROCESS... 125
CHPT 17 THE BLIND SEE... 137
CHPT 18 CHURCH HURT... 143
CHPT 19 NUGGETS & PEARLS... 151
CHPT 20 HE IS...YOU ARE... 163
CHPT 21 THE AWAKENING... 167
"AWAKENING" PRAYER... 175
PRAYER OF SALVATION... 177
SCRIPTURAL REFERENCES... 179

ACKNOWLEDGMENTS

First and foremost, I thank God. I give Him all praise, honor, and glory for everything in my life. I pray that this unexpected assignment bears much fruit, for only He and I know the depth of His Long-suffering towards me. He is my very breath, and without Him, I am nothing.

Overwhelming gratitude, respect, and admiration to my beautiful Mother Louise, who unconditionally loves me, and has always been a significant source of strength and support in my life. Thank you Mom. I love you beyond words.

A special thank you to my pastor, Bishop Henry B. Fernandez of *The Faith Center* in Sunrise, Florida, whose leadership and vision have taught me about "crazy" faith and how to move mountains.

To Prophet Ezekiel Williams, who also mentored me and under whose tutelage I grew exceedingly, I offer my sincere gratitude and appreciation for the many seeds sown in my life.

I would be remiss if I don't mention my "Viragoan" circle, which encourages me, supports me, and regularly prays for me. From my heart to yours, thank you Deborah Burnett, Sheila Chambers, Barbara Lampley, and Cathy Russell. I love you ladies and greatly appreciate you all!

A special acknowledgment and thank you to Sheila Chambers for the many prayers and conversations that carried me through. God's abundant Blessings to you always, "my beautiful sister from another mother."

To my sons, Billy and Chris—words can't describe how grateful I am to God for blessing me with the two of you. There is no end to my love. May you both walk in the calling ordained for your lives by God. May you each run your race and finish your course with excellence, so that God's glory shines in and through you for all to see.

Lastly, sincere appreciation and special thanks to Dr. Belinda John and the entire Divine Works Publishing team for their invaluable guidance, patience, and expertise in perfecting this work. God's continued blessings.

PREFACE

Everyone has a story to tell. We each have our own crosses to bear in life, and usually, they're related to words we've spoken and/or decisions we've made along life's journey. My personal journey probably isn't more extraordinary than anyone else's. I've had my share of trials, disappointments, and failures, just like you. Reflecting on it all now, every struggle I went through, every battle I survived, every lesson I learned, taught me something valuable, and developed my character—the very core of who I am.

There is nothing like hands-on training… And the School of Life was my teacher! The consequences, repercussions, and the scars I carry all stemmed from those experiences; but so did my strength, tenacity, and wisdom. To look at me, you wouldn't know that I've experienced some of the things I'll share here, but "looks" never tell the full story.

Like many women, I've gone through the challenges and heartaches that come with broken relationships. Here, I will share one such experience that was pivotal in my life. It devastated me and almost destroyed me. Although I didn't know it, at the time, it marked a major turning point for me; yet it is my cornerstone. Had it not been for the Lord on my side, *everything* would be totally different! I'm not just saying that, I mean it literally. GOD saved me! From what? Let me be direct: it was *God* that sustained me during that devastating time. It was *God* that prevented me from losing my mind. It was *God* that stopped me from committing suicide—and homicide! Yes, I said "homicide." It was *God* who protected me and delivered me from the enemy's hand. It was *God* alone that loved me and brought me through it all. Had my flesh prevailed, I'm truly not sure where I would be now.

My hope is, sharing all of this will minister to someone who has ears to hear and eyes to see. 2 Corinthians 1:3-4 (KJV) says, "Blessed be God, even the Father of our Lord Jesus Christ, the Father of mercies, and the God of all comfort; Who comforts us in all our tribulation, that we may comfort them which are in any trouble, by the comfort wherewith we ourselves are comforted by God". Paraphrasing my understanding of this scripture, since by the Grace of God, you survived your battle, that which you learned and experienced is to be shared with others as a testimony, to comfort, help, heal, or encourage them during their own time of trial.

It's possible that none of what I will share here applies to your life. Maybe you've never experienced any of the trials in my story. If so, to God be the glory! But, if I identify with just one person, and help them in any way, then I will count this assignment as a success.

In the end, my main point is this: **GOD IS A GOOD GOD; A FAITHFUL GOD!** And if it wasn't for God's love for me, someone else would be telling this story.

(Disclaimer: This is my personal experience. Since this was almost 20 years ago, the dates and events discussed are based solely on my recollection of them.)

INTRODUCTION

I remember a renowned bishop visited our church one year. In his sermon, he talked about certain pivotal moments or events that had such an impact on him that they altered, or had the potential to alter, the very course of his life. As I sat listening to him intently, I recalled one such event in my life, in which I was rocked to my very core for years. Had God not intervened, instead of living this present life, I would have changed the course of my life forever! In other words, things could have easily gone another way, a much worse way. Except for the Grace and Mercy of God, they didn't. Because of Him, this is a testimony of triumph instead of a life's tragedy.

Like many Christians, I was under the impression that once I got saved and accepted Christ as my Lord and Savior, everything would be "perfect" in my life. I didn't understand the various trials and struggles I'd face in my new walk. At that time, nobody told me about the *other side* of this walk—that hell would break loose in my life! No one said that everything that worked before would no longer work! That problems would arise from "nowhere," and that everything that used to be simple would become overloaded with complications! No one informed me that I now walked around with a permanent bullseye on my chest, back, and head for the devil! It would take several years to understand that this faith walk is not for the faint of heart. It takes time and vigilance to mature in faith. I learned that after Salvation, the *real* fight begins.

Hopefully, my transparency will minister to you somewhere along your own faith journey. Perhaps it will help you out of a hard place, or prevent you from getting trapped in one. If you find yourself anywhere in this story; whatever it brings to mind, be it recent or past, I want you to know that those mishaps, mistakes, and misfortunes don't matter. *Nothing* you have done or failed to do makes any difference. Give *all of it* to God! He loves far more than I can explain to you, and I guarantee that won't change with your story. **You** were already *His* decision before the foundation of the world (Jeremiah 1:5). *You belong to Him.*

I'd like to open with an experience I had that is not directly related. I will skip through parts because it is not the pivotal event I want to share, although it certainly could have been one. Its purpose is to help you understand my frame of mind then, and to help you know the lengths the enemy will go when he knows that a heart has truly turned to God.

CHAPTER 1

THE SETUP
Laying the Groundwork

It was over 30 years ago now, I was a postal employee, working the late night shift. I was married but quite unhappily. My husband was having an affair and had been for a while. Yes, I knew about it—it was hard not to, since all three of us worked in the same area. My co-workers could hardly wait to share such juicy gossip, so "conversations" were constantly circulating around me. I had already determined that it was only a matter of time before I left him and filed for divorce, but I had unknowingly complicated the matter. I didn't know how to hear God's voice then, nor did I understand His way of doing things.

Let's go back. My relationship with this man spanned the course of many years prior to our actual marriage. Before I was saved, we had been dating a few years and had a great relationship. But Salvation changed me, and he didn't like it one bit. Like most new converts, I was on fire for God! The things I used to do, I no longer desired to do. God was Who I talked about all the time! I read my Bible, went to church, bible study, conferences, conventions, anywhere to hear the Word. I was hungry. I listened to sermons and gospel music on the radio constantly. I was even in three choirs at church! I was bubbling over in love, and my affection for the Other Man was obvious. Eventually, I was given an ultimatum: him or God. I remember thinking: Really, what kind of choice is that? Who competes with God? And why couldn't he see that this was a good thing? Long story short, I chose God and the man I thought I would marry, left me.

My heart was broken and I was miserable. For a while I struggled with that decision, even though I knew it was right. But there was still so much I had yet to grow to understand in this faith walk. Is it supposed to be like this? Aren't I supposed to be happier now? I felt confused and alone. I didn't understand what was happening. I kept thinking he'd miss me, you know, "couldn't live without me" type thing. I thought he would realize he made a mistake, but as time went by, that didn't happen.

Over a year later, we talked about getting back together, but that didn't last. The conversation always ended the same way—my heart belonged to Another. Because we remained cordial and somewhat flirtatious from time to time, within a couple more years, he came back again. Nothing had changed but we talked. A little at first, then more and more. It seemed this "break" had changed things. We admitted that we missed each other and that the love was still there. If we were going to get back together, I felt there was nowhere else for us to go but marriage. He agreed. He knew I wasn't giving up Christ; and I promised not to push him too fast to accept Him, (with the understanding of course, that he actually would). So we married. We pooled our finances and went after "the dream". We bought a house, cars, new furniture—everything we desired. We had already been together on and off for about 10 years so we made up for lost time. It was exciting! I was happy, he was happy, and I could finally see the "good life" I thought came with being saved, coming together. Fast forward…bickering, problems, the affair.

Then, I think seventeen months later, I would be served with divorce papers! I was taken aback at first because I thought that I would be the one to do that, especially with his affair. I should have rejoiced, but I was saddened by it. I felt like I was sucker punched twice: you cheated and you don't want me. *Wow!* Despite this, something didn't feel right but I couldn't put my finger on it. I kept trying to pinpoint what

> *HE said, "Conversion was never on his mind, revenge was."*

was bothering me when I heard God speak. HE said, "Conversion was never on his mind, revenge was." Huh? First, I thought I was trippin' because I heard *Someone* talking to me when no one was around. After realizing it was actually God speaking to me, I needed to comprehend what He was saying. God then gave me the revelation about the whole "reunion" thing between us. HE explained it was a set up —a ruse! That my husband had no intention of accepting Christ or staying with me! He was paying me back for choosing God over him several years ago. The plan was to leave me in deep debt, take half of everything, and get a large cash settlement by forcing the sale of the house. That realization slapped me so hard in the face! At first, I just couldn't believe it. I couldn't accept that. This man loved me; God was mistaken!

It was a huge pill to swallow, but I'm so grateful God stepped in to protect me in that fight. I won't go into great detail because it doesn't matter. This is what I want you to understand. God had already saved me once from this man years ago. However, not understanding that, I put myself right back in harm's way. Remember when I chose God over my Ex and he left me the first time? That was the blessing I did not see or understand, but God knew! He's Omniscient. He knew the end from the beginning, and He knew *that* man's heart meant evil towards me.

Note: Some people are in your life for a reason, some a season, and some a lifetime. Many people will come and go, all with a purpose; either they bring blessings or they bring lessons. When a person walks out of your life, the way my Ex did, their season is usually over. But before declaring that you can't live without them, ask yourself: What was their deposit in your life? Did their presence bless you? Were you better because they were around? Did you prosper in any way? Or were you hurting most of the time? Troubled? Insecure? Is your life calmer now that he/she is not in it? Are you at peace? Did you learn something?

In my case, and often in male/female relationships, when a man leaves a woman, she feels rejected because she didn't initiate it and has no control. It's a negative reflection on her directly and activates a defense mechanism full of emotions. I had to face the fact that I invited him (and that mess) back into my life. I didn't really know to ask God about it back then; I didn't know He even cared. But even if I had, I thought I knew my Ex better than God did. You might say, I thought I knew better than God!

I understand now that I was blinded by lust. Not sexual lust. I'm referring to any fleshly (earthly) desire that goes against God's word or causes us to question the basic common sense God gave us. In relationships, logic and reason flip flop in our heads, and we adjust our minds to fit our desires. We make changes, excuses, and often ignore the warning signs. We think we'll miss out on something, so we allow people and things of the world to entangle us, causing us to lose our way. We don't honor God the way we should, so we fall into traps and pitfalls repeatedly. Not realizing, our relationship with Him is the one to be cherished, nurtured, and protected. No one or any thing should ever come before Him! God is a jealous God (Exodus 34:14). "I am the LORD. That is my name. I will not give my glory to another; I will not let idols take the praise that should be mine"(Isaiah 42:8 NCV). There shall be no other gods before Me (Exodus 20:3). We often test God's love, not fully comprehending it. But there is no Greater Love! We like to think that we can accept Jesus and save ourselves from hell, but still live in this world doing whatever we want to do. We use Grace as an excuse, thinking God will understand our humanness, but it doesn't work like that! The same way

Christ traded His sinless life to save us, we traded our sinful lives for that Salvation. He took our unrighteousness, we took His righteousness. He took our weaknesses, we took His strength. He took our sicknesses and we took His healing. We took His holiness for our unholiness. And He died a death that you know you would never want to. So no, we don't just get to renege and be selfish. Everything we needed to get back into right standing with The Father was given to us by Jesus at that Great Exchange! If we belong to Him, we should desire to change for Him. We should want to be more like Him, but we are selfish people! Thank God, because He is a loving and gracious God, slow to anger and plenteous in mercy (Psalm 103:8).

I was saying that God had previously saved me from the very mistake I found myself in for the second time. After that revelation, I knew I was in trouble. You can imagine as word of the divorce spread, things became increasingly difficult for me at home and at work. Maintaining my mental and physical health was cumbersome. Then something happened. I do not remember consciously making the decision, but I began to pray more, read my Word more, and seek God more. I focused on Him and not my situation. It brought me peace and quieted my emotions. My walk with God changed in the midst of my struggle. Gradually the pain of my circumstances began to ease even though nothing had changed outwardly. I just kept asking God to help me. I repented, admitted my culpability, and asked God to forgive me. I told God that I understood this "mess" was my own doing,

> *I repented, admitted my culpability, and asked God to forgive me.*

but that I needed Him to help me get out of it.

Getting served with divorce papers hurt me but I came to understand it was God giving me my way out of the marriage. So why was I feeling guilty? Why did I even care? He was the one cheating! Lying! Stealing from me! Did he really want to throw everything away? What did she have that I didn't? I flip-flopped in my own mind, confused and pitiful, despite my talk with God. But God had exposed him. Ex was a patient man—cool, calm, and calculating. I'm sure he had done his research. In a state where community property entitlement was 50/50, I guess he figured he had committed to a fake marriage long enough to collect. He was coming for the spoils. Most everything we owned was in my name. I didn't care about the material things, but the house was different. It was my home! I would have purchased it alone had he not come back into my life when he did.

Since then the laws for divorce may have changed, but at that time, unless you outright owned something before marriage, (including money), and could prove it, it was considered community or shared property. With community property, the monetary value is equally split between parties unless there is an agreement stating otherwise. With most smaller material items like furniture and TVs, an agreement could easily be reached with few problems.

For us, the more valuable assets were retirement, cars, properties, or other financial streams. Those larger items have to be sold unless one of you has the financial means to pay the other their fair share of its value. Because of that, our divorce had the potential to be messy. But God showed up!

During the purchase of our home, my Ex had to sign a quitclaim deed putting the house solely in my name because his bad credit would have skyrocketed the interest on our purchase (a quitclaim deed is a document that states a person is giving up their legal interest or claim on a property). That is what God used to save me! That quitclaim gave me the leverage I needed in court, and protected me from having to sell the house to give him half! Technically he could have fought it, but the lawyer's fees alone would have been astronomical, and he knew I would have fought him to the bitter end. Oh he was a sly one, but he didn't fool my God! God had perfectly orchestrated that plan in advance to protect me from the onslaught that lay in wait for me in the upcoming years. While I thought that quitclaim deed was for one purpose, God meant it for another altogether! I was looking short term at a lesser interest rate on the mortgage, but God sought to protect my future.

I did have to settle with him, but what he received was a pittance compared to what he was after. Because of God, I emerged victorious from that battle. God knew my heart and He knew the heart of my Ex. What the enemy meant for evil, God turned it for good (Genesis 50:20).

I was done with men! Don't want one. They're all the same – take, use, take, use! I was still hurt and had some recovering to do, but as buzz of the case circulated, I was the peacock strutting at work. Not in an arrogant way. I was proud and happy my God had defended me. I learned something about God from that (Ex probably did too).

I felt important, loved, and stronger inside. I had been recompensed, and grew even more zealous in my pursuit of Him. I thought I had a better understanding of the "faith walk" and wanted to serve God with my whole heart.

 When we don't honor God the way we should, we fall into traps and pitfalls repeatedly.

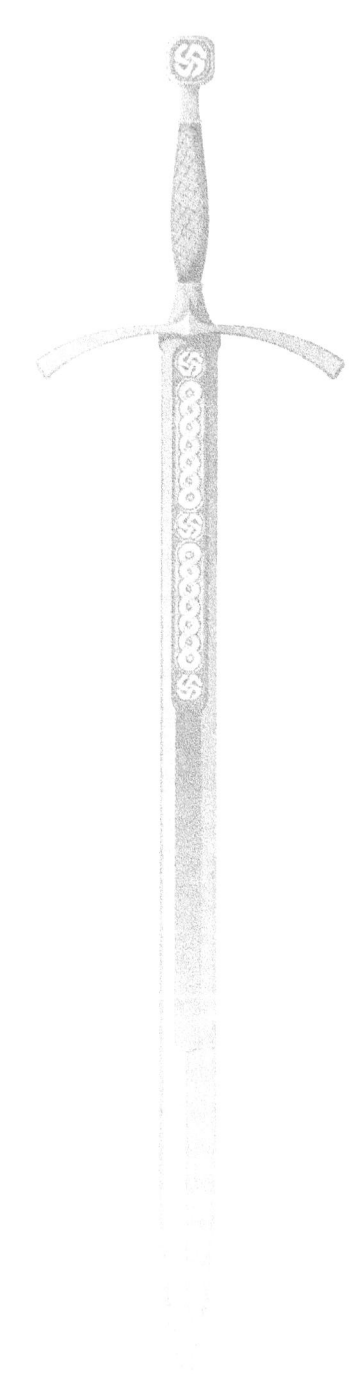

CHAPTER 2

THE ASSIGNMENT
A Call to Arms

After that fiasco, I found solace in music from a radio station in our area when at work. This station played all the great oldies as well as the popular top R&B hits. The music kept me preoccupied and energized—regularly helping me get through the night shift. One particular night, I was very tired and listening on my headset awaiting the next up-tempo song to shake me out of my drowsiness. A slow song came on instead. It was a song I was familiar with but definitely not what I wanted to hear. I remember thinking I could make it through the next few minutes in hopes that the one after would be the one worth the wait. I don't remember what the slow song was now, but the DJ played it over again! I was disappointed but thought that maybe he fell asleep or had to go to the bathroom and didn't make it back in time, so it repeated automatically. I didn't know, but trying to figure it out stimulated my mind long enough to get me most of the way through the song again. I was slowly crashing, but pressed my way through with high anticipation of a series of "party songs" sure to follow. Finally the song was ending for the second time and I heard his voice. I didn't actually pay attention to what he said, but hearing his voice put an end to all my speculation about him no longer being in the studio. He wasn't on the mic long. He made some reference to the song title because I heard its name, then just that quick, he was gone. I thought, *Great, let's get the party started please!* What I heard next left me in complete shock and disbelief. He played that same song a third straight time! *What the heck is going on here? Am I trippin'?* I looked around to see if anyone else was listening. *Is anybody else hearing what I'm hearing? Who is this guy?* I was furious and wanted to complain to someone, needed to complain to someone, but of course no one would be in the corporate offices till morning! Ironically, I realized I had the very energy boost I had been looking for. Towards the end of the song the third time, I calmed down because I knew I had no control in this situation. *Just ride it out.* When I heard it for the *fourth* time, I realized this man was in trouble! As I honed in on the words, the song expressed his pain and what he could not speak. Now he had my attention in a different way, and I began to pray for him. I didn't know exactly what was wrong, but by the content of the song, it was "relationship" trouble. I felt really sorry for him and asked the Lord how to help him. I don't recall God saying anything, but this man, whoever he was, had left a definite impression.

I thought about him the next day—how he must be hurting, and I prayed for him a second time. Again I asked the Lord how to help him. Having just come out of my own situation, I could relate. I found it did my soul good to have something else to focus on, especially because I saw my Ex every night. I didn't hear from the Lord, but maybe I was the only one who had read between the lines. I felt like I should do *something*, I just didn't know what.

> *I didn't hear from the Lord, but maybe I was the only one who had read between the lines.*

During my shift, I found myself expectantly awaiting the late night DJ to come on. I wanted to hear his voice and assess how he was doing that night. I hoped he was feeling better. Maybe he had even resolved his issues. I was in a state of high anticipation as time moved closer and wondered if my prayers had worked.

He sounded much better and I was satisfied that I contributed to that. I remember thinking, *how interesting that I was praying for someone I didn't even know.* For the rest of the week, I called myself monitoring his speech and behavior. *Maybe things were resolved.* His attitude seemed to have improved. He even had a great sense of humor. I found myself laughing at his on-air antics, and liked his personality. Relieved, I had found an escape from the gossip I still encountered every shift.

One night he was on the air taking requests. I called in for a song I heard on the station before, but didn't exactly know the name of. He asked my name but I gave him a fake one because I had heard him poke fun at people before. He would jab pretty good too, not in a bad way, it was usually funny. I remember getting a good laugh several times before, but I wasn't going to be the brunt of any joke, so my guard was up. After that set of songs, I called back to scold him about labeling some other song as my request. That's when I found out he didn't know the song! He tried to explain but I saw the opportunity to take a jab at him, so there was shared playful banter between us. To his credit, the next night he found the song and played it, specially dedicating it to "me," (that is, my alias). I heard it and called to thank him. He was easy to talk to, and we laughed a lot. After that, we spoke a couple times each week. Sometimes I'd call in to try to win a contest. Other times, he would randomly just dedicate a song to me, prompting me to call.

Soon, a couple nights turned to every night we worked. Within a couple weeks, we felt like we had known each other for years. Eventually our conversation made it around to the night he played that record four times in a row. I was right about the relationship problems. It seems he had marital problems too, but there was a factor I had never considered. He was suicidal. It was hard to accept that this person I listened to, laughed with, and now spoke to almost every night, had lost all hope. I thought of how people regularly interact with each other, yet never recognize another's cry for help. I prayed that this was only a passing thought he was experiencing, but I felt I now understood my assignment. I didn't know if he knew Jesus, but I knew he needed to, or at the very least, get reacquainted. He was in danger in more ways than one, and I needed to help him get on track.

As we continued to talk, I learned that he was a believer in Christ and attended one of the major churches in the area. I was familiar with his Church's name and its Pastor, so I knew he was under sound doctrine. I was able to incorporate faith into our conversations. We discussed the issues troubling him. I shared with him as well. It bonded us in a way that allowed us to be vulnerable with each other but not judgmental. It was a good feeling, and I had a new friend.

 When we don't wait on God's instructions we risk derailing our assignments and ourselves.

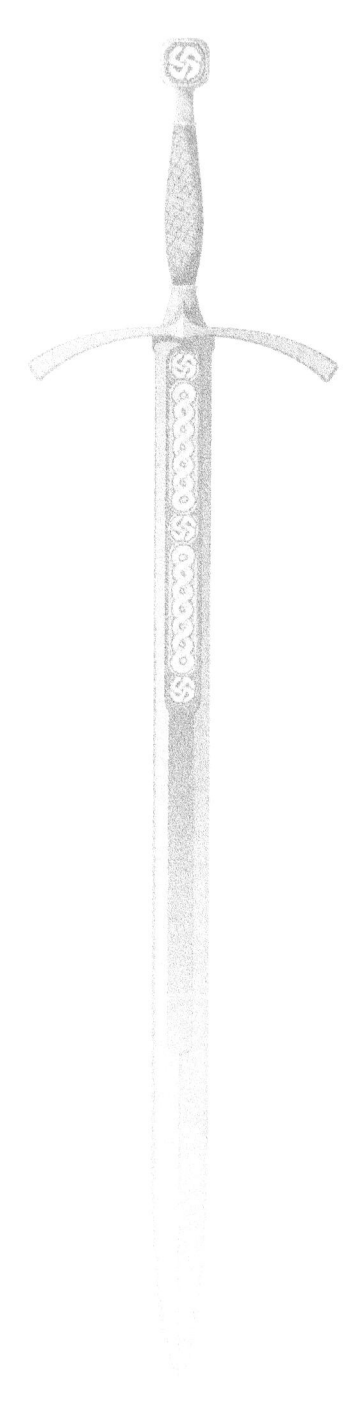

THE ENCOUNTER
A Stealth Alliance

The Lord was included regularly into our conversations after that. We talked about scripture, our churches, and the different ministries in which we served. We had a lot in common. He sounded happier now, stronger; *maybe he needed a new friend too.* I remember thinking that his suicidal thoughts seemed to have dissipated. I was pleased, feeling I had a hand in that.

After about a month, we decided to put faces to the voices we had been hearing. We agreed to meet at his workplace, because my shift was over first. During the drive there, my heart was pounding. On the phone, we were just two people talking. But, this was not that and I was nervous. I remember several thoughts running through my mind all at once. I kept asking myself about the nervousness but couldn't concentrate on one thing long enough to answer any of my own questions! I wondered if he would still like me after he met me; if he would still want to talk to me on our shifts at night. *Wait. Here I am, on my way to meet a complete stranger in the middle of the night! Nobody knows anything about it, and I'm worried he won't want to be friends any more? Had I lost my mind?* I was definitely trippin'!

It was a short ride at that hour, so I was there rather quickly. He had given me instructions on what to do once I arrived, and before I knew it, I was standing in his presence. He turned around in his chair and motioned the "shhh" sign by putting his finger to his lips, because he was on the air and the mic was open. *Well, he doesn't look crazy.* I *felt* OK, so started looking around the room filled with records, tapes, and blinking lights. I had never been in a studio before so I was taking it all in while I waited. He turned again and stood with an outstretched hand to introduce himself, but not the regular way. He didn't tell me who he was, he told me who I was. He said, "You must be Monique." My mind said *"What?"* I was instantly insulted and shocked! *Did he just call me by some other Chick's name?!* Oh, I copped an instant attitude inside! It hadn't crossed my mind the whole time we spent talking and sharing with each other on the phone that I never told him my real name! He still knew me as "Monique," the alias I gave him the night of the song request. Having figured it all in those few seconds, I then made the split second decision to let him keep believing that. Now that I had actually met him, before I exposed my *true* identity, I wanted to see if *he* was really the person he seemed on the phone. (Funny right?) *If we decided to cut ties right then why would he need to know my real name?*

He was nice looking—tall, about 6'3", good build, well-groomed, with a short haircut and goatee. His pleasant smile was inviting, so it felt good to finally put a face to the voice I had become so accustomed to. First impressions are important so I tried to relax. He didn't seem nervous at all but I wouldn't have known. We made small talk as he quickly showed me around the studio, explaining all the gadgets and buttons. I got to witness the "signing off" process as he introduced his final song for the night before bidding his audience farewell till "the same time tomorrow." The phone lines lit up like a Christmas tree as fans tried to get a final word in before he left. He had a smooth voice and seemed to truly enjoy what he was doing. I remember admiring that, thinking what it must be like to captivate an audience for several hours every day. It was intriguing. And just that quick, it was all over. By the time we reached our cars, we were talking and laughing like we were used to on the phone, and I was at ease again. The time zipped past, and saying good-bye was comfortable and non-threatening. It was a positive encounter and I felt we both parted with confidence that our meeting had been a good decision. The ice was broken, and all seemed well.

Our friendship continued growing, and there was a certain freedom between us that usually took people years to develop. We "trusted" each other and talked about almost everything. Eventually I told him my real name, and boy did I catch it on that one! I knew I should have said something sooner, but it's true, the longer you wait to admit fault, the harder it is. Needless to say, that was a long standing joke between us for a while. We had matching wits and humor, which I really liked because a very large part of me is quick-witted. It's funnier and more gratifying when a joke doesn't have to be explained to be understood.

Our serious discussions had to do with life issues like: marriage, kids, jobs, and finances. I was absolutely in no position to talk about marriage, but I did share my recent experience in a bit more depth. We talked about our careers, and griped about people and issues at our jobs. He was experiencing real financial struggle, so I was willing to try to help get his spouse a job at my company. The pay was enticing, but the hours were long and the work was very physically demanding. I knew not just anyone could meet those qualifications, but I left the offer on the table for the future.

Our common ground was discussing kids and finances, so those were regular topics. What parent doesn't like to talk about their children, and who couldn't use more money? Our kids were always the highlight of our conversations. Mine were a few years older than his, but all the stories were entertaining. We shared countless "kid" stories, laughing, because the innocence of young children is always pure, raw, and hilarious.

Now if you were a fly on the wall, you might surely think that "Peter and Paul" were real family members! Whether recovering financially from divorce, or falling thousands of dollars down the annual pay scale all at once, is hard to grasp. That's what happened with him. Venting helped, but no one wants to start over, especially after you've reached a certain age and milestone in life. The idea of working so hard to achieve a comfortable level of security then losing it all in a moment's time, is unimaginable. The mind won't readily accept that kind of devastation. The shock of it is too overwhelming.

As he told me the story, I imagined a toddler using his blocks to build a great structure. He takes his time carefully picking and placing each individual block, trying his best to coordinate balance, height, and weight until his masterpiece is complete. Then with just a few more blocks to add, his older brother comes and in one swoop, knocks the whole thing down so that even the foundation was shaken! The toddler is shocked and immediately reduced to tears, not knowing what else to do. (It may take him time, but he will begin to build again.)

Note: I fully understand that starting over later in life is devastating. But, you cannot give up! The Bible tells us in Ecclesiastes 3:1-8, that there are seasons to everything in life. There is no set age limit that prevents us from catastrophe. We may not be completely prepared but we should be aware. Nothing in this life should ever knock us out permanently—not when God is for us. When your foundation is built on The Rock, the rain, the floods, and the wind may come, but the house will stand (Matthew 7:26-27).

> *The Bible tells us in Ecclesiastes 3:1-8, that there are seasons to everything in life.*

No matter what happens you *will* recover. So have your temper tantrum and get it all out, then start to build again! The scripture says to give thanks *in* everything. Your attitude will make the difference. So Pray. Fast. Trust. It will be difficult, but nothing is impossible with God (Luke 1:37)! Soon you will hear, "Behold I will do a new thing; now it shall spring forth; shall ye not know it? I will even make a road in the wilderness, and rivers in the desert" (Isaiah 43:19 NKJV).

His story made me feel much better; good in fact. I experienced *nothing* compared to him! Hearing what someone else is going through, has a way of putting your own life in perspective. That's when real insight and understanding step in. I silently thanked God because I wouldn't have wanted to trade places. Listening to my Friend, my battle was ending, but I realized his was just beginning. He confided that divorce was inevitable now, having exhausted "all" options. I was sorry to hear that, especially with what I recently went through. I only knew to pray for them.

Eventually, our conversations spilled past our work hours. When we weren't venting, it was nice having intellectual conversations, and hearing different perspectives on things. I enjoyed the mental stimulation and the challenges. I even helped him with ideas for his radio show.

One afternoon, we had lunch and I found he was rather popular around town. I was a little impressed at what I saw and heard. I chuckled to myself because before that infamous night of DJ'ing, I didn't even know he existed! Now it seemed "everywhere" I went, I heard his name. I smiled inwardly because I actually *knew* the man behind the voice. He was a friend of mine.

 When your foundation is built on The Rock, the rain, the floods, and the wind may come, but the house will stand.

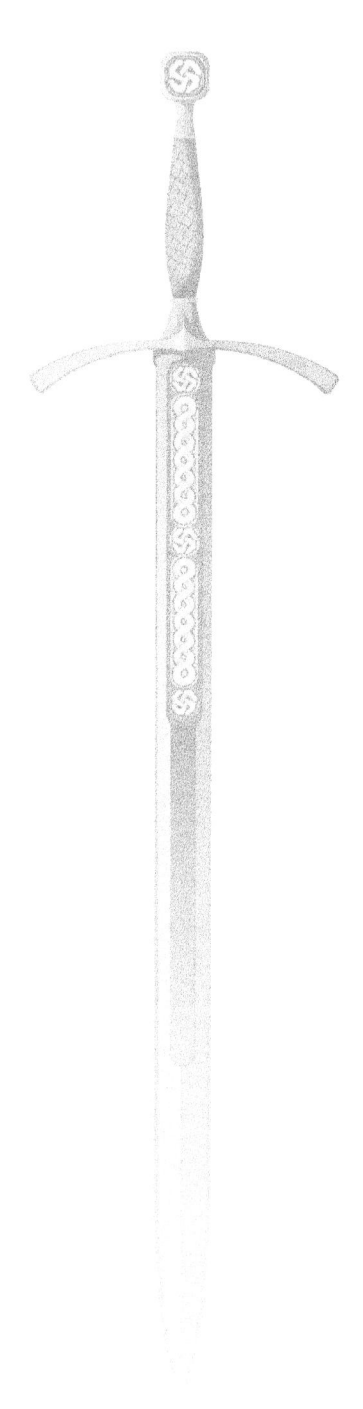

CHAPTER 4

THE BREACH
Lowering the Guard

It happened one night at the studio. I was visiting and we had been laughing and talking like we often did in between his sets. I don't remember the exact date, but I can remember other details about it. I needed to use the restroom but didn't know where it was. I was standing against the door on the inside of the studio facing him, awaiting directions, as he sat at the controls. He held up one finger meaning, 'give me a minute because a break is coming, then I can show you'. As soon as the mic was off, he got up to direct me through the hall. He walked towards me. His hands were on the door, straddling both sides of my face just a little above my head, as if to push the door open, but he didn't. (I remember feeling really small with him so close, looming over me. He was practically one whole foot taller than me and easily 100 pounds heavier. For a brief moment, it could have been quite intimidating or threatening had I not felt I knew him). I looked up at him questioning the hesitation. His eyes locked on mine in a very different way, and all in the same motion, he leaned over and kissed me. In that split second, every warning bell rang and every siren sounded in my head! Stop signs popped up everywhere and my mind was screaming, "Nooooo, what are you doing!?" But then I noticed heat in my body and a little light headedness, as my stomach instantly filled with butterflies. I had a split second to make a decision on how this would go... So I kissed him back. It was a sweet tender kiss, that spoke volumes without any words. I can't say how long it lasted, but almost twenty years later, it's still etched on my memory. My heart fluttered and all clarity escaped me for a moment; you know the kind of moment when you're not sure if you're awake or dreaming? It was a moment like that. I didn't realize it then, but it was the first in a series of pivotal events I would face.

  The following several months were extremely blissful as we became everything to each other. We were together as much as time would allow with our different schedules, or we talked on the phone in between. It was an awesome time in my life and I was happy! As the other processes in our lives were still taking place, we found strength and comfort in each other in every way. I was moving further and further away from God but I didn't see that. I was still serving in the church. But now I felt like I had a real partner to forge through life with—somebody similar to me, who understood me; somebody *saved*, who had my back—a "soulmate."

Note: There is something important I want to discuss so let's stick a pin right there. Because of its depth, there could actually be a separate book written on these subjects, but here we're just going to graze the surface of both.

The word *soulmate* is a created secular word that is defined as a person ideally or perfectly suited for another person, as a close friend or romantic partner. It is not limited to that definition, but the word is rarely used when speaking of a platonic friend. Rather, it is mentioned of one involved in a romantic *physical* relationship between two *unmarried* people. The word is not found anywhere in the Bible, nor does it have any biblical connection. It is my opinion that it's an attempt used to justify the sin of fornication, while hoping to attach some spiritual meaning because of the word "soul"; but it still doesn't have any. *After all a soulmate should care about your soul, not just your body right?*

On the other hand, there is something known as a *soul-tie*. This word is also not found in the Bible and is more of an implied biblical term. It's defined as a deep *emotional* bond between two people, usually formed through sex, thus linking them together *spiritually*. The two are similar, but the ungodly soul tie is more damaging because of its long term effects on the soul and spirit of a person, not just the body. From a biblical perspective, the soul, which is composed of your mind, will, and emotions, would be the place where this bond takes root, because it emotionally ties one person to another. Let me explain.

Sex is the most intimate and sacred act created by God for humankind. Its purpose and significance surpass surface knowledge and have a much deeper meaning than what it has been reduced to. Sex was never meant to be the meaningless "feel good" act it has evolved into today. It is a *gift* from God, meant to be a beautiful bonding and solidifying of a marriage, conjoining two people together. It is through this act that two individuals become one, by the complete surrendering and intertwining of one's spirit, soul, and body with another. It is sacred, and it is holy.

Marriage is a covenant, which God instituted between a man and a woman. It is this union that excludes *all* others from the relationship, and joins the two of them together as *one*. The Bible states it this way, "Therefore a man shall leave his mother and father and cleave unto his wife, and the two shall become one flesh" (Genesis 2:24). Jesus said it Himself in Mark 10: 7-8, *"For this cause, a man shall leave his mother and father and cleave unto his wife; And they twain shall be one flesh: so then they are no more twain, but one flesh."* This is the **holy** bond of matrimony.

Now by definition, marriage could be considered a soul tie because of the physical, emotional, and spiritual binding and bonding of two souls. Howbeit, this would be a Godly soul tie, ordained by God, fulfilling His intention and purpose for marriage.

The opposite to that of course, would be an ungodly soul tie - the binding and bonding of two souls through adultery or fornication, (sex *outside of marriage*). This kind of bond gives the devil "legal" access into one's life because of sin. Through this intimacy, demons and generational curses can be released and transferred. Not only are two sleeping together, but every partner either of them has *ever* had are now partners too! Permission of everything ungodly in either person, or their bloodline, now has free access to pass between the two. Stepping outside of God's designed purpose is dangerous and costly.

Whatever is contrary to God's Word or His way of doing things, has already been twisted! We can't make sin right because the world condones it. The Bible says in 1 John and Romans 6, that all unrighteousness is sin, and the wages of sin is death. As children of God, living contrary to His word places us outside His hedge of protection and unlocks the door to the enemy. Proverbs 14:12 (NKJV) says, *"There is a way that seems right to a man, But its end thereof are the ways of death."* Now, it's not speaking directly of physically dying, (although in today's society with disease running rampant that is a real possibility), but it's speaking more of the death or destruction of the soul and body. Iniquity, or willful sin, will separate us from God and cause us to stay outside of His perfect will for our lives.

See, we are **spirit** like God, made in His image and likeness (Genesis 1:27). We live in a physical **body**. It is the body which houses or encases our spirits, the same way a garage holds a car. I previously mentioned the **soul**, comprises the mind, the will, and the emotions, thus making humans a three part being. Think of a peach. A peach has an outer skin or covering, the flesh or edible fruit, and the pit or seed, found in the center of the peach. Even mentioning these parts individually, most people have an idea of what I'm referring to. Although each part is different with its own characteristics, the three parts together constitute what most understand to be a "peach". So it is with every person - three parts together, body, soul, and spirit, make up a human being. Comparing our three parts to the peach, the outer part of us is the body, which is the skin of the peach. Beneath that is our soul or the inside part, and our spirit is the pit. Notice the pit is the innermost part of the peach and is *protected* by two other layers. Why? Because it is the core of the peach, similar to the human heart being protected by layers of muscle and the rib cage. Let's go deeper.

Have you ever seen a broken pit inside a peach? If so, you know a smaller "stone" is inside. Well that stone or seed, is the actual life source of the peach. It's the real heart of the fruit. It is in that seed where reproduction and growth lies. If *that* seed is corrupted in any way, it could stunt the peach's maturation, mangle its flesh, or completely mar it's appearance, ruining all potential. Liken this to a child of God. Ungodly ties, damage or harm the physical body, manipulate and control the emotional soul, and hinder the development and maturation of the spirit.

Picture a tall, clear glass of water. The glass represents the body, the liquid represents your soul, and its transparency or clarity, represents your spirit. The benefits of this water are numerous: it's odorless, colorless, refreshing, and it's extremely healthy for your body. But regardless of these benefits, a plain glass of water is "boring" to you. So you add "ice," (the sin of fornication). Now the water looks more appealing. It's enticing and you're imagining how it'll feel to the body going down (lusting). The Spirit of the Lord is already telling you not to indulge, but you don't want to hear that. You take a sip. Then another. And another. It's good and you like it.

After some time, the ice begins melting, but you don't care because the water still *feels* good going down.

Then, you notice *something*. It's not obvious at first because the ice was clear like the water, but as it continues to melt, it becomes more evident. A thin film forms on the surface of the water, co-mingling with the ice. You shake the glass a bit to be sure you're seeing correctly, and the film begins to separate. Some particles sink to the bottom and settle, others float in the body of the water, and some remain on the surface, clinging to the ice. The water isn't pure anymore.

That film represents sin. You may not notice the effects immediately because you cannot physically see them. You're simply enjoying the feeling, *(surely that's not hurting anybody)*. But your spirit and soul are becoming more and more tainted; and you have no idea what you're getting entangled with.

Sex outside of marriage is not God's will or His way. With each encounter, you lose more of yourself. The Bible says in 1 Corinthians 6:18-20 (ESV), "Flee from sexual immorality. Every other sin that a person commits is outside the body, but the sexually immoral person sins against his own body. Or do you not know that your body is the temple of the Holy Spirit within you, whom you have from God? You are not your own for you were bought with a price. So glorify God in your body."

> *Every other sin that a person commits is outside the body, but the sexually immoral person sins against his own body.*

Just like the particles and sediment in the glass, the residue of this sin "mingles" with your soul and spirit. Like clarity dissipated from the water, so it also does from your thinking, your righteousness, and your holiness. The more you indulge, the less bothered (convicted) you are, and the less you hear the Voice of God. You've turned a deaf ear and your heart is hardening. God's hedge of protection leaves and different spiritual attacks enter. The dots may never be connected, because you're only thinking carnally. It could be one thing or a combination of things like: sickness, financial struggles, job problems, family or children issues, even depression. Every area that was once blessed is now blocked, and you have no idea how or why.

Think about this. Once you see that film and sediment in the glass, would you continue drinking the water? Would you still want it? Chances are you wouldn't. You'd throw it out, and probably gargle or brush your teeth. The point is, it should bother you. ***Check and see if you have missed the mark somewhere. Are you still aligned with God's will?***

It's much easier to be in denial than to admit bondage. No good thing lies outside the will of God. Make the move back to your heavenly Father, from Whom every good and perfect gift comes. ***Confess, repent, and start again.*** We have a God that loves us with a perfect love. He keeps loving us even through our indiscretions and our iniquities. He's always calling and wooing us to come back to Him—to let Him in to be the center of our lives. He *truly* loves us. Though we willfully sin against Him, He is full of Compassion and Grace. His love toward us doesn't change. Jeremiah 29:11 (NKJV) says, "For I know the thoughts I have toward you, says the LORD, thoughts of peace and not of evil, to give you a future and a hope." God's heart is *always* for us! He is Gracious, Merciful, and Just. The bible warns that He is not to be mocked (Galatians 6:7). God is sovereign—to be referenced, praised, and honored. I'm not sure where it originated, but I want you to think about this saying I heard. It resonates deeply inside my soul every time I think of it. It says: **Grace** *keeps giving me what I don't deserve, and* **Mercy** *keeps me from getting what I do.*

Now, I was saying that I was happy; that perhaps I had found my soulmate. The months whizzed by, and before I knew it, a year had already passed. It was a great year too! Considering what I came out of and where I was now, was incredible! I felt I deserved some happiness…. and I was loving it! Bae was now in the midst of his battle and we were pressing through together as a team. There was an uneasiness inside me, but I ignored it. It was subtle, but strong enough to get my attention from time to time, and make me uncomfortable. I didn't know what it was, but inwardly, I had a suspicion. I didn't ask God because I was happy and wanted to stay that way.

I found his career held many perks that the average person would not be privy to. I had access to free concerts and went to "celebrity" events. I could even walk into a clothing store and leave with free items if he mentioned that store's name on the air. That impressed me! The cost of airtime versus the cost of those items was incomparable, so that worked in my favor every time. When my shift at work changed, we'd attend events at local establishments on a regular basis. He would call me at the spur of the moment and tell me to get ready for the evening. Sometimes I knew where we were going and sometimes I didn't, but it never mattered. He was well received everywhere we went, and now, so was I. People liked us, gravitated towards us, and complimented us. We looked good together, and matched wits, intellect, and conversation with almost everyone. We had a certain je ne sais quoi. We knew how to work a room, playing off one another in banter or jest, or even finishing each other's sentences. We were a great team and people took notice. I was truly enjoying this new aspect of my life. My past debacle was a fast fading memory. I rarely noticed the uneasiness inside anymore. It would still surface because God was still trying to get my attention, but I wasn't listening. My ways were moving me further and further away from His perfect will for my life.

 Ungodly soul ties, damage or harm the physical body, manipulate and control the emotional soul, and hinder the development and maturation of the spirit.

CHAPTER 5

THE FIRST FIGHT
A Familiar Foe

Sometime in our second year together, he lost his job. I don't remember when it was, but as you can imagine, it was quite impactful. He still had bills to pay, a hefty mortgage, and kids to support, all with no new money coming in. The pressure of maintaining a lifestyle he could no longer afford was crushing. His divorce was not final yet, so there were limitations on what he could do. He fell into a slump rather quickly because he couldn't find a job and nothing he tried was working. His confidence took a nosedive, the money waned, and the prestige was gone. It was difficult for me too really— watching someone you love in pain. I did my best to be positive, keep him encouraged, and be supportive. I felt this was a passing thing, but I had trouble keeping him convinced of that the more he was rejected. In the back of my mind, I was concerned those suicidal thoughts would creep in again. I couldn't allow that, especially not on my watch. I was consumed with trying to fix this and find answers that would resolve this whole issue and get things back on track. In the meantime, I did my best to keep him motivated and strong.

I remember it was one of his daughter's birthdays. He was distraught because he couldn't give her a party like she asked. So what did *I* do? I stepped in. "Daddy" gave his daughter a beautiful birthday party with the works: decorations, balloons, cake, ice cream, and the like. It was a great little party for short notice! Seeing the joy and excitement of those smiling faces (his and theirs) was enough to put a smile on my face too!

Another time, I really wanted to go to a concert to see a performer neither of us had ever seen before. I was hoping it would be an enjoyable evening out for the two of us, perhaps take his mind off his troubles for a bit, but I knew he couldn't afford to take me. So what did *I* do? I bought these great tickets but gave them to him along with spending money for our evening, just in case we ran into people that recognized him while we were out. How others viewed him was very important to him.

I did many things like that trying to hold everything together. I didn't want him to give up. I prayed too, because it was what I knew to do - though I was so off course, my prayers were probably bouncing off the ceiling.

Over the years, Bae had shared many stories with

me about his previous career in the music industry before DJing. Talk about juicy stuff—those stories about the industry were fascinating! He had quite the collection of memorabilia too; gifts and tokens he'd been given over the years from various artists. Then an idea came to me that I felt we overlooked. (I actually thought it was a God idea). He had "connections"; a rapport—he knew people! Surely, *someone* along the way would help him out, or perhaps owed him a favor. It took a lot of convincing for him to ask any of them for help. I understood his pride. I knew that was a major issue for any man, but desperate times called for desperate measures, right? Cutting to the chase, that's eventually what happened. He contacted a few people, but only got one offer—to DJ in Miami, Florida.

I said, "Florida?"

"I know," he said, "but what else can I do? There's nothing else for me here. It's not like I haven't been trying. I've got to do something to make money."

"No, I know that… Just, Florida? That's all the way across the coast," I replied.

My real issue was not so much where the job was, but what that meant for our relationship. I had done the "long distance love thing" before, and it didn't end well. I waited to see if he would bring the topic up himself. Either way, would speak volumes to me. To my delight, he began to lay out a sketchy plan for our future. So from then on, we began to discuss relocation and rebuilding (neither of which I cared for, but he was my man, my future, and my "happily ever after").

Our new challenge brought a combination of anxiety, anticipation, and apprehension. There was much to do before leaving the state. We were regularly racing the clock. It was a big ask and a big task, but I knew we could do it together.

Bae would be leaving his children behind, which was heart wrenching. Adding that to the pressure of starting over, and a long distance divorce, pending an unknown settlement, was a heavy weight to carry. He, (we), had no idea what to expect.

For me, I had a steady career, and two children in high school. My oldest would be graduating and leaving the state for college in summer, and my youngest would be graduating the following year. I didn't think it was right to uproot my youngest in his senior year of high school, so I made the decision to stay in Cali one more year instead of leaving that year with Bae.

The ride to the airport was bittersweet, but we tried to make light of the situation. I think we both had unspoken fears of our own, masking them in order to protect the other. We'd been together a couple years now, and Bae and I had been inseparable. We had fought and conquered most issues together. I viewed this temporary separation as another bump in the road.

However, my real struggle was internal. I was still quite unsettled about a long distance relationship. I did not like the idea of separating for a whole year. I realized my emotions about the subject had been suppressed all those years. I had not forgotten. And although I felt more secure in this relationship, that past experience began rearing its head. I was now battling baggage I didn't know

Truth is a powerful weapon

I had. I argued (with myself), *"But what is love without trust?"* So pushing those feelings aside, I was determined to work through it. It wasn't right to hold him responsible for something someone else had done. I didn't want anything to interfere with building a future with the man I loved *now*. And oh did I love this man!

Time was moving slowly and quickly. Slowly because it was hard to be separated from him for such an extended period of time, and quickly because there was so much to do and so little time to do it. My body was exhausted, but my mind would not allow it to break down. I was driven by sheer will and determination, so I continued to push on.

By the second month of his move, I was visiting, and attending my first South Florida party. It was a meet & greet actually. A couple of the listeners decided it would be a good way to corner the "new Kid on the block" so they could rightfully accept or reject him. When we arrived at the venue, there was a huge poster welcoming him, on which guests could sign or message. There was food, music, and a nice crowd of people waiting. All went well and he gained some new fans. It was a kind gesture, greatly appreciated, and good for him. For me, I was laying groundwork for potential future friendships. It was a win-win.

His new condo was a bit lacking however, so I bought things he needed but didn't yet have the money for. I did what I could to make him comfortable. After all, it wouldn't be long before I would be there too.

He had to return to Cali occasionally because of the divorce, but he still had friends there, and of course, I was there. We often joked about the frequent flyer miles we were racking up. The more we visited together, the more excited I became about the relocation.

In Cali, the divorce got messy and things started changing for him. You know when the phone goes straight to voicemail when you call someone? This was his experience no matter when he called to speak to his children. He hadn't spoken to them in a while and there had been no attempt made to contact him even after he left messages. Father's Day came, and there was no call, no message, no drawings, or homemade arts and crafts projects sent, nothing. He was distraught. It was clear there wasn't going to be *any* communication from the girls. His heart was broken. So...what did *I* do? I explained to him that things happen: plans get pushed back, things get lost in the mail, delays occur, and the sort. I convinced him to wait a little because I believed *something* was probably on the way. I don't know that he bought that exactly, but I then went and bought two age appropriate Father's Day cards, signed them both with my left hand disguising my penmanship, and mailed them to him. Oh the joy, when those cards arrived! He was ecstatic and couldn't contain his excitement. He was bursting at the seams when he called me, describing the cute little cards to me and how the girls had written their own names! (I never did tell him it was me).

Another time I was on a "stakeout" for him. I actually "followed that car" like a scene from a movie! Because I was still in California, I was called upon to put my detective skills to work. (Ladies, you know those *skills* we possess when we're out to catch *someone doing something?*) Well, I was on *that* case. I remember staking out the area. It was hot that day and I had been waiting a while. When my chance came, I was on the move. You should have heard me talking to myself, "Don't get too close"; "Speed up, you're gonna lose 'em"; "Uh oh, red light, red light! Stop or go, stop or go? C'mon make up your mind!"

The first time I lost my mark because I stopped for that red light. But failure was not an option. On the second try, I "closed the case." I have to laugh out loud when I think about that. Absolute madness! Oh the crazy things we do in the name of love.

 Removing God from our decisions grants the enemy access to deceive us.

A NEW JOURNEY BEGINS
Steering the Sunshine State

His former trials were over. It would only be a short time before he was back on his feet. Bae was settling in. I could tell by his speech he was more at ease. He had always been funny, cool, and likable, now I could hear those traits returning. His fan base was growing rapidly, and once again, I was entertained with the many stories he shared. I was happy and excited for him. I felt I was one of the last pieces to complete the puzzle; and of course, we now needed a new church home.

Several Sundays we talked about the various churches he visited looking for a suitable place. In Cali, we both had pastors that delivered the complete Word of God.

However it took this experience to understand all churches are *not* the same. According to the teaching, *any* church just won't do. The spirit man is hungry for the Truth of the Word and needs to be fed the same way your stomach growls and rumbles when your body needs nourishment. Not only does the church need the foundation of The Word, but it also needs a Pastor that fears God more than people. The Word needs to be anointed in Truth and power, so that you can be well rounded in your growth and maturity in Christ.

Then it happened! He was really excited to tell me but the three hour time difference seemed an eternity. He had found (us) a church he felt at home in. I was happy and excited, but anxious to visit to check it out for myself. (I was stronger in my faith walk then, so this church needed *my* approval).

The church was an hour away from the condo. It was a nice size church with a second floor balcony. There were Greeters at the door and a lot of chatter in the lobby before service. The men introduced themselves without hesitation, but the women were tripping over themselves trying to get Bae's attention! I received more "glares and stares" than "hellos and welcomes." It was a bit amusing watching these groupies' behavior, still I tucked it away in the back of my mind, reserving judgment. We sat in his "section," which was to the right of the pulpit. A few congregants came to speak, but I knew they were really coming to be nosy. I played along, but was more interested in observing the atmosphere of the church.

The choir was good. The Presence of God was ushered in and the atmosphere set. I was in the choir at my church, so the thought crossed my mind as a ministry I'd like to join when I relocate. Then the Pastor came out singing. *What, the Pastor can sing too!?* He had a voice similar to Marvin Sapp's! I loved hearing him! But most importantly, the Word went forth with anointing and power. Bae had done well.

I had the chance to meet the Pastor personally after service. Bae introduced me as his "rock"—he was so very proud at that moment (and I was immediately overwhelmed with love). The Man of God was cordial, pleasant, and told me he heard a lot about me. I reciprocated the same. He revealed knowledge and excitement about my upcoming move, as we assured each other we would not be strangers. It was a brief chat with promises of future ones to follow, but others were waiting to speak to him, so we took our leave. I was relieved and pleasantly pleased. Everything seemed to be falling into place.

> *Everything seemed to be falling into place.*

While visiting, whenever Bae and I were separated, we stayed on the phone together. I would "work" his whole shift with him! We discussed ideas, possible contests, and information we thought his listeners might want to know about on his show. Again, I was a "random caller" as we experimented. In the evenings, we would go to his favorite restaurants, or a venue where he needed to make an appearance for work. People were getting to know him—and know me too. It reminded me of our days back in Cali. *Sigh...* time to head back.

In December my kids and I were headed across the coast to spend Christmas with him and his son, who would also be visiting there. His son was closer to my boys' ages, so they were good company for each other and got along well. I had already mailed gifts ahead so they could sit around the tree. We brought the rest with us. It was wonderful! We exchanged gifts, went to the movies, played games, stayed up late laughing, joking, and watching television. I felt I had gotten a taste of what our family life would be like together and I was loving it!

We dreaded separating, but the kids had school and I had to work. I tucked those precious memories away in the rolodex of my mind, smiling, and reminiscing the whole way home. I was over the moon, and could hardly wait for our new life together to begin.

 The Word needs to be anointed in Truth & Power, so you can be well grounded in your growth and maturity in Christ.

RETURN TO BASE
Irons in the Fire

No time to dilly dally. Upcoming sports games, plays, proms, and yearbook events filled my agenda for the spring semester. I worked as much overtime as I could because there were always two to do for. Whatever one did, the other did. You would have thought I had twins! Nevertheless, I had never deprived them of anything (within reason) and I wasn't going to start now that they were at the door of graduation. There was one more year to get through after this one, then I could rest. All the hard work, the sacrifices, the challenges of being a single parent, would soon be behind me because they would be beginning their own journeys towards adulthood. I was relieved and terrified at the same time. Like most parents, the idea of letting "my Baby" go on his own was difficult. I questioned whether or not I had done enough, if I could have done more, perhaps done things differently? Was he prepared? Letting go was hard. Although I hid them, the thoughts were constant in my mind. *Had I been a good Mom?*

Only a few months more for the oldest now, so I had to know I did my best. I had raised two young men without a Father. I taught them manners, respect, honor, and integrity. I promoted education, took them to church, kept them safe and comfortable. I did better as I learned better. But in all this, never once, did I see the plank that was in my own eye!

> *Never once, did I see the plank that was in my own eye!*

June meant graduation. Much of the family flew in to be a part of the celebration, and Bae flew in from Florida. It would be my family's first time seeing and meeting him, although they knew his name. His outgoing personality meshed well, but time passed too quickly.

Now that graduation was over, it was time to prepare for college. I agreed to let my oldest enjoy the rest of the summer with his friends before they all went their separate ways. We would do all our "college" shopping in that state once we arrived. Since we had to fly there, that made sense. I should tell you that my son was attending a private college in – (wait for it)… Miami, Florida! I couldn't help but think God was blessing me. Another piece coming together, especially concerning my children! I was much more comfortable knowing Bae was there since my son would be all the way across the coast without me.

Simultaneously, I had been working on my career move too. I had no idea how long it might take to find, but I needed a job transfer! Well, not exactly a transfer; what I needed was a swap. After 22 years of service on my job, I was not willing to simply relocate and start from the bottom climbing the seniority ladder again. A swap would allow me to switch facilities with a fellow employee in a similar position but not lose any years of service. Finding a swapee that wanted to come to my particular vicinity in Cali wasn't difficult, but the tricky part was finding one that had more seniority than I did, so I could maintain all my current benefits.

During a swap, both employees assume the seniority date of the junior person, so I needed someone with more years of service than I had, that way I lose nothing. Seniority was very important when it came to job bidding, weekends, holidays, and vacations. I was finally in the top 20% in my building and wasn't willing to start over. The search was usually tedious and intense. Many were looking to swap, so it was a race to make first contact with any potential match. To my surprise, it didn't take me as long as I thought. I found someone who had two more years seniority than I, willing to wait the extra year I needed to allow my younger son to graduate! It had only taken a couple months, and I was overjoyed! We agreed to meet in August when I brought my oldest son to college. I was to tour his facility and get an idea of the route and traveling distance from Bae's condo. Then he and his wife would come to Cali and chart out similar information for their needs. We were both relieved and excited we were a match. Now, it was time to start the paperwork.

I wasn't praying much at all, I was busy and too preoccupied. As every step worked out, I took it as a sign that I was headed in the right direction; that God had heard me and was honoring my previous prayers.

 The Lord is with you, while ye be with him; and if ye seek him, he will be found of you; but if ye forsake him, he will forsake you. 2 Chronicles 15:2

A RISING STORM
A Brewing Undercurrent

College life here we come! We arrived in Florida Wednesday night before the busyness of college the next morning. This was to be a "business" trip for me. Time was of the essence. We began early in the morning. We toured the campus, dorms, met counselors, filled out paperwork; all things that come with college orientation. It was mid-afternoon now and we were in our last line waiting to finalize the financial aid. Something was happening. I was out of my element so I wasn't sure what I was sensing. Chaos? Stress? Maybe anxiety? I didn't know but kept trying to figure out what was going on. Then I began to hear chatter and I understood.

There was *urgency* in the air! Katrina was coming. Hurricane Katrina that is! Being busy and tired, I hadn't heard about it, so it wasn't on my radar. The school was beginning to talk of shutting down, and so were many of the processing areas. We were in our last line, but still had a few people in front of us. I wasn't sure what I was supposed to do. Financial aid paperwork isn't a quick thing. Even if we left the line, we had to wait for our ride, so I decided to stay to see if we'd get processed. We made it! My son now had his school ID, class schedule, books, cafeteria vouchers, dorm room, and his financial aid. God came through again. Now it was time for *us* to get home! Others were understandably trying to complete their processes too, before being cut off. I felt for those out-of-state kids that had no parents there - possibly their first time away from home. They were alone, and a hurricane was coming. How terrifying! Scurrying and panic invaded campus. My son and I witnessed a complete change in the atmosphere. Because of what was happening around us, we began to feel a bit anxious too. It was time to go! We waited, somewhat impatiently, for Bae to come get us for almost an hour! I couldn't understand what was taking him so long; he was already off work and wasn't that far away. He gave me some flimsy excuse, but my growing anxiety of the impending danger made me forget to revisit that. We had earthquakes in Cali, but this would be our first hurricane. Watching and listening to others had made me somewhat edgy. I knew a Category 5 was not good. Thank God it landed in Florida as only a Category 1. Still, the winds were howling at about 80 mph, all electricity was lost, and there was death and destruction across the state. *Everything* was affected! I remember seeing debris everywhere.

There was no phone service—almost all communication was down; no a/c—the humidity was insufferable; no ATMS—if you didn't have cash, you were in trouble; and very few gas stations were open—without a full tank, you weren't going anywhere. Finding food and/or water was nearly impossible if you hadn't stocked up.

I hadn't considered it much in Cali because I was never directly affected by an earthquake. Earthquakes are unpredictable, but there are essentials to always have on hand. I had an epiphany here though. Katrina had been talked about…a whole lot! Not knowing how long systems would be down, preparation is key. I understood the importance of water, packaged food, batteries, candles, gas, and cash. *If* a restaurant or store *could* open, only cash was accepted. I rarely carry cash! This was an eye-opener and quite surreal.

During life's storms preparation is key

To this day, I'm still grateful to God that Florida's damage was minimal.

Bae had to work because the radio was the main source of communication and information at that time. The station would receive calls from all around, then announce all the pertinent information to the people over the airwaves. They'd relay emergency information like areas to avoid driving, information on power outages, which restaurants or stores were open in a particular area, and with what service(s). I saw people on the streets grilling and selling hot dogs, hamburgers, sausages and water. I was offended the first time I saw it. *The nerve of these people capitalizing off others' misfortune,* I thought. I shook my head in disgust and disbelief. But then it hit me! How many times had I heard it said that in the midst of chaos and crisis, there is still opportunity? *"Those people"* had prepared for just that, and were seizing their moment. The parable in the Bible of the ten virgins came to mind (Matthew 25:1-10). Am *I* prepared? (Are *you* prepared?) It was an "aha" moment of revelation, and I unexpectedly learned another valuable lesson—sufficiency or deficiency? In every circumstance, your level of preparation directly relates to your outcome.

Within a couple days, most places were open for business. So on Saturday, Bae and I headed north about an hour to find where I would be working. Because of the safety factor, I wasn't able to enter the facility, but we met my swapee and his wife for lunch to discuss our future plans. The four of us got along well, and we were able to agree on the terms and expectations of our swap.

Despite Katrina, it was a productive trip. I returned to Cali believing my son was going to be fine, and having survived my first hurricane. I had also cleared another hurdle, securing my swap for next year without any loss to me. I felt good and had a sense of accomplishment. I could see my "to do" list decreasing, but there were still *big* things that remained: selling my house, packing, transporting my car and belongings, getting my youngest son set for graduation and college, not to mention Christmas was around the corner. All these had one major thing in common: MONEY! It was gonna take a lot of money to get all these things done.

My *new* normal work day was 12 hours, with only one day off, but I would work seven days when allowed. When permitted, every one of those hours was double time and a half, with weekend premium pay! My body was being abused and I was physically and mentally exhausted, but I had a goal to complete with a deadline that couldn't be altered. I was focused and determined, much like an athlete that pushes their body to the brink, then gets that second wind. I kept God tucked away in the back of my mind, believing it was Him working behind the scenes for me, and moved my own desires to the forefront, (a form of idolatry), telling myself that I could make up the time with Him later. Except for my routine Sundays at church, the quality time I spent with God was all but gone, yet I never noticed.

 In every circumstance, your level of preparation directly relates to your outcome. Are you prepared?

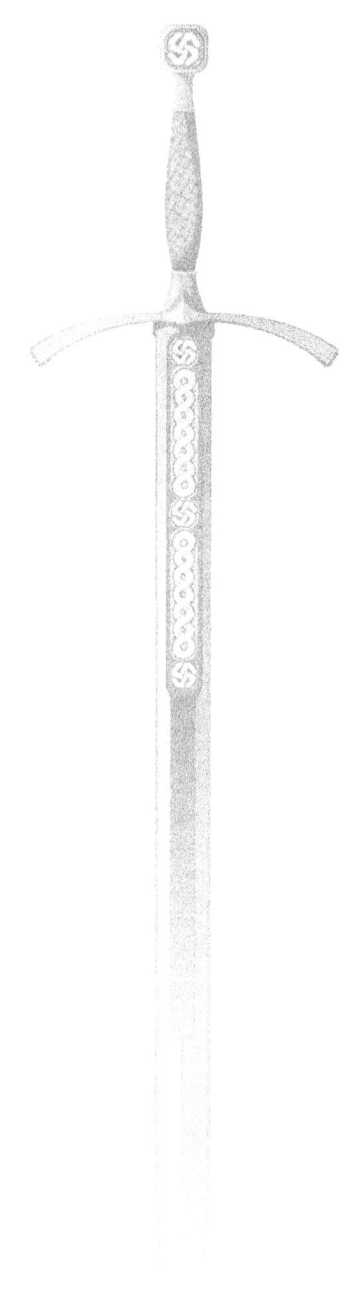

CHAPTER 9

A SURPRISE ATTACK
Friendly Fire

December rolled around quickly. I have a large family, so that year, my kids and I traveled to my home town to be with them. I asked Bae to come with us. It was a big deal because I wanted him to meet the rest of the family that didn't make it to my oldest son's graduation, and experience what our Holiday celebrations were like. He informed me that he would be in Cali spending Christmas with his daughters. It had been a while since he'd seen them so I understood that was the priority. He explained the plan was to split some time with their mother, so he was excited! The closer it got to Christmas though, the more unsure he sounded about the reunion. I thought it was settled, but it seemed things kept changing from day to day. In the end, he saw the girls but not for very long, and nothing had worked out the way he had hoped. He felt he spent money he hadn't really had, with very little to show for it. He was back in Florida before Christmas even came. Whenever we spoke on the phone, I could hear the disappointment and sadness in his voice, and he could hear the joy and excitement at our house. He tried to conceal his pain, but I could feel it. It hurt me to see him hurting that way, especially around the Holidays. So… what did *I* do? Of course, I came to the rescue! He had already been invited to be a part of our Celebration before, so I simply re-extended the invitation. I felt it was important to keep him at a safe distance from pity and depression, rather than to allow him to wallow alone for several days with his own thoughts. It took some convincing on my part, because he didn't have any money, but I did it, so I bought him a ticket. It was the last of my money too, but all expenses were covered because I was at home with my family. Plus, this put my original plan back in motion.

    He arrived mid-morning on Christmas Day. After all the introductions and traditional breakfast call, my Mom casually asked him about his accommodations. I felt my eyebrows furrow a bit because it was such an unexpected question that seemed to come out of nowhere. Not sure what to make of that, I was immediately agitated and defensive. I jumped in, and within moments, a huge argument broke out between my Mom and I! My mind was reeling! I couldn't believe what I was hearing: '*Where is he staying*'? *Whaddumean? You already KNOW where he's staying! Exactly what is going on right now?* The questions were rolling in my head one after the other. I was beside myself! Then I realized she was the messenger, and something had happened to cause this sudden and unexpected turn. I had my suspicions but they were irrelevant at that moment. I thought, *"How are you just gonna flip everything? And why didn't you say something **before** Bae arrived?"* I was shocked, embarrassed, and raging mad all at once! My fight got ugly, but my Mother was the target since she was the messenger. In order to try to calm the situation, Bae said he would go stay in a hotel. I glared at him, speaking without ever opening my mouth! *"Now where are **you** gonna find a hotel room on Christmas Day that doesn't cost an arm and a leg?! And where was **that** money coming from, because you sure don't have any!"* Neither one of us could pay anything at this point. I was livid! My Mom kept trying to calm me down, but I wasn't having it! I couldn't believe my ears! There was really no talking to me. I was out of control; beyond reach. Full of righteous indignation, I announced we were leaving, stormed out and went downstairs to pack my things.

All the family was at the house now except for my oldest sister and her husband, but I didn't want to be around anybody. Everything was ruined for me and I just wanted to leave! My sister and brother-in-law are habitually late so I figured Bae and I would be gone before they arrived. I was in my room when the phone rang. From what I understood, they were en route but the snow was slowing them down. *Snow?... Whatever!* About twenty minutes later the doorbell rang, and the commotion began upstairs. They had arrived and the chatter was ongoing about their journey. Apparently, the snow was falling so furiously that they skidded and slid

59

all the way to the house. The streets were slick and driving conditions very dangerous . The forecast called for heavy snow continuing throughout the night. A "no travel" advisory was issued because of low visibility and quick layering on the streets. Although I was downstairs, with that news, I heard my Mom declare that no one was leaving. She announced that *all* of us were staying there that night! I thought, *"Oh, so now what? Now the "rules" change again? Now **you** have a say? Humph."* Though unforeseen circumstances now tipped the scale in my favor, it didn't matter one bit. My ego had taken a severe hit. I was humiliated and angry. *I would rather take my chances out there than to stay here with them!*

Oh, how quickly the enemy steps in when the door is opened! The enemy saw a great opportunity to use my anger to his advantage. My head could have exploded with false pride. I kept shaking my head saying, *"What a way for him to meet my family. The nerve! I'm so embarrassed!"* I simply couldn't wrap my head around what had happened. My guard had been down completely. I never saw it coming, which made me even madder! If anyone else had reacted in the same bad manner I did, there's no telling how out-of-hand the situation could have gotten.

> Oh, how quickly the enemy steps in once the door is opened!

Eventually, my Mom came downstairs to talk to me, in her sweet way. She's always been a peacemaker and came to me in humility and love, even though I was the one that was wrong. She's the type who will take the blow for someone else to calm a situation and find a favorable resolution to bring peace. There she sat, very passively, in the room with me. Her sweet soothing voice, wooing me in her loving way, apologizing, for her part in the fiasco, both past and present. She's not perfect, but she has *always* been an extraordinary example of 1 Peter 4:8b, which says that love covers a multitude of sins. It's difficult for the enemy to compete with that kind of love. He loses his foothold because Light will always conquer darkness. Likewise, my Mom's gentle spirit would always break through the strongest of walls because of her meekness and humility. She lovingly said what she had to say, then left me to think about it.

Thus an appeal had been made, and I had a decision to make. The fight within was real. I was struggling with pride and wanting to be vindicated. *Surely you know it's not that simple!* Nevertheless, because of the unconditional love of my beautiful mother, I made the right decision to let it all go. My anger slowly dissipated and I began enjoying my family. I made the rounds introducing Bae, who was warmly greeted and accepted. Everyone made a special effort to act as if nothing had ever happened. There was love all around. It was a beautiful thing, and I was happy because of my family's grace.

One of our traditions is playing games. It's a big thing for us, and all of us are competitive! Whenever a newcomer is invited to a family gathering, they're forewarned about game night. The family likes to see what the newcomers are made of, so they're thrown straight into the deep end. Kudos to them if they can swim in the deep, but if they sink, the wall of shame awaits. They will always be reminded and teased about their "inabilities", and so will that family member. Well, Bae was a pro and fit in perfectly! I was proud, and once again happy to be home enjoying my family. The "incident" faded somewhere into the background. It turned out to be a great Christmas, and I thought, *so everything really is working out beautifully.*

 The unfading beauty of a gentle and quiet spirit, is of great worth in God's sight.

CONFRONTING CONFUSION
Facing the Unknown

I had eight months left to get everything done. I was both excited and afraid at the same time. When May arrived, I received a beautiful card and gift for Mother's Day from Bae, but my heart melted when I saw the "Mother-in-law" Mother's Day card for my Mom included. She and my sister were already with me in Cali, helping pack for my big move. He even sent a shout out to them on air. I was ecstatic! It was so thoughtful, but more importantly for me, it solidified our plans to be married, and meant Bae would be family.

With my Mom and sister both there with me, I could rest. I needed to save my leave at work for the transition, so I was really happy to have them. The house was getting its makeover, they had the chance to meet and interact with my realtor, and my swapee and his wife made their visit to Cali during that time. It was still busy, and there was never a dull moment. I was so grateful for my family! My Mom did all the cooking while she was there. She and my sister did everything; all I did was work and rest. By the time they were done, what remained were things only I could do like: finding a transport company, selling the house, preparing for my second son's graduation and college move, etc. There was still pressure because of the time constraint, but I could see light at the end of the tunnel. I would definitely need the break to recuperate before beginning the job again in September.

    After May, Bae and I talked less frequently. He was quite popular in Florida now, regularly making appearances and hosting events when he wasn't on the air. I was a workaholic, and still "Mom," so our schedules often conflicted. I missed our conversations but I was determined to stay on schedule. We had an agreement. *Just stick to the plan—it's almost over.*

    I still attend church every Sunday, but mostly out of habit. I wasn't going to Bible study or singing in the choir anymore. I had truly enjoyed the music ministry and sang with some famous people over the years, but without that commitment, my time was immediately consumed with other things. I felt I'd get back on track eventually, but I pacified myself at the time with, *"God knows my heart."* I did believe that because of how well everything was working out.

    June brought prom, pictures, and graduation for Son number two. I did my best to ensure he had everything he wanted on his special day as well. Although it wasn't as big or as busy as last year's, it was still a nice celebration. As before, I agreed to give him the remaining part of the summer to enjoy with his friends before leaving for college. This time, we would both be leaving the familiar for new beginnings. I was less stressed about the college process though, having been through it the year before. I knew what to do and how to get it done, so I believed everything would go smoothly. This son would go to Georgia, and I was fine with that. I would be in the same state with one son, and less than 24 hours away from the other. I felt relieved to be much closer in proximity to my family in Maryland too, instead of all the way across the coast. I found it brought me a level of peace I had never thought of.

When July rolled around, I was running on fumes but pushing to meet the deadline. My list was almost complete: my son would be heading to college and settled before the move, my swap was finalized so I had a job, the movers and the transport company had their dates and were paid for, and I already had my airline ticket to leave. There were minor areas to attend to, but the only major feat left was the selling of my house. It was on the market and generating good interest. I was hoping to get a buyer and have the paperwork done before I left the state, so I could be free of any binding ties in Cali. I didn't want to have to travel back and forth like Bae did.

When Bae and I did talk, he seemed different—somewhat detached. His speech was not the same, nor his attention towards me. A thought hit my mind. Something stirred in the pit of my stomach but I suppressed it, blaming stress and nerves, although I never completely dismissed it.

Something was wrong.

August was to be a big month for Bae and me. His girls would be visiting for the month, and I would be arriving in a couple weeks. We decided we'd need to plan a vacation with the girls, get a routine established, and look for potential areas where we might want to live. It was an exciting plan for the month!

I was shocked to find my house in a bidding war for over half a million dollars, but of course, I was tickled pink! It was between two bidders in particular but the deciding factor was the difference in deposit. My realtor advised me to go with the bidder that put down the higher deposit. Now I was set! I would do whatever it took before leaving to try to keep the sale on track. I knew to allow for complications, but I wanted to close before the Holidays started rolling around. Woohoo, everything was finally coming together!

I was so excited! I could hardly wait to share the good news with Bae. His divorce was now settled, and a sale like this meant there would hardly be any struggle for us going forward. We could get married, purchase the house we wanted, and begin our new lives together. All the memories I kept in my heart since our Christmas with the boys, began swirling around in the forefront of my mind. I was bubbling up inside, overwhelmed with enthusiasm and joy.

You know that "fairytale dream" girls have growing up, where Prince Charming comes and sweeps you off your feet; then you live "happily ever after?" Well, that was never my experience. Pain and heartache were not strangers to me, so I no longer had stock in that dream. But now I allowed that "happily ever after" to resurrect in my heart. The mere thought of being so close had me on cloud nine! I had actually found my Prince Charming! He loved me and I loved him. Together, we were *invincible*. We could weather any storm because of our love and respect for each other. We were best friends, and had been through some tough tests already. I believed in my heart, we could do anything! This was only the beginning! Oh the heights we could soar together! I am so blessed!

When I finally had the chance to tell Bae about the house, I didn't get the reaction I thought I would. He *acted* excited, but he wasn't really. I knew him. Immediately, my mind flashed back to the "college incident" the previous year. I didn't like it. I didn't want to jump to any conclusions unnecessarily, so I tried probing a bit to see if I could get some understanding of this reluctance. He knew me too, so he remained aloof. We began to bicker. Every word was scrutinized, misinterpreted, or misunderstood. Then something burst forth. He announced that he and the girls were going to take a cruise the same week I was to arrive! *Wait, What!?* He went on to say that he was overworked and stressed, and would have very little time to spend with the girls, who would have to return to their mom "shortly." Not sure if my ears were deceiving me, I repeated what I heard for clarification, asking, "*You're taking a cruise with the girls,* **without me**, *the* **same** *week I'm due to arrive?*" Yep. I had heard correctly. Immediately, the red flags began popping up in my head. I automatically remembered that other long distance relationship. Instantly, I searched my mind for every "suspicious" conversation we ever had since he left Cali. I felt nauseous and angry at the same time. The questions began firing off my tongue in rapid succession: *Why* *wouldn't you wait for me to come before a cruise? You don't want me with you guys? What are the dates for this cruise again? So where have the girls been then while you're at work every day? Who's taking care of them? Who's picking me up from the airport? How am I getting to the house? You asked a total "stranger" to get me?! Really? I haven't even seen you since December! What, you've moved into a new place?* My mind staggered in unbelief as my conscience screamed obscenities. I was blindsided a second time (the first time being that Christmas with my Mom) and it infuriated me! I'm not sure what took place after that. I don't remember much of what was said. My ears couldn't hear, my eyes saw only red, as I desperately tried to regain control of my emotions…and of my mouth. I'm sure we got off the phone after that bomb, because the rolodex in my mind opened up. Every date, moment, name, and flimsy excuse, replayed in my head. *Everything was suspect!*

    Little by little, I began to connect some pieces together that previously had not made sense to me, and I didn't like what I saw. In another week, I would be leaving everything I knew; everything I had established in my own adult life. My house was on the market. I sold many of my appliances, I'd given away much of my furniture, the movers were paid, and I had given up my position at work. Now, it all appeared to hang in the balance. *Was this a mistake*? I didn't think to pray because my head was messed up. It took me a moment to process and absorb what my heart and head fought about. I was conflicted in my emotions. On one hand, I didn't want to believe what my head was saying, but on the other hand, I couldn't deny it either. This was a familiar feeling; something was terribly off. The more I thought about it, the more agitated I became! I was worked up and couldn't relax. I called him again, and asked him directly: "I'm not sure what's happening here… Do you still want me to come or not?"

He should have expected it, or maybe he was surprised by the authority in my voice. He answered, "Yes," without hesitation and with a hint of annoyance that I would pose such a question.

I was ready to fight but his answer quelled that. As we talked, there was a calmness in his voice that began to lower my defenses. He began to explain himself, and there was a semblance of the man I knew. I was still leery but I *chose* to relent. I heard a famous pastor once say, "My inner me is my enemy." Truer words were never spoken. I was conflicted inside as my mind and heart battled for supremacy—the battle to believe what my gut was yelling, or to accept what my heart wanted to believe. Inside, every red flag imaginable erected in my mind: WARNING! BEWARE! DANGER AHEAD! STOP! TURN BACK! But my heart did not want to accept that. I immediately began to think of our history together, our partnership and love, and all the plans we had made. I made

> *Against my own intuition, I acquiesced.*

excuses to settle my busy mind: *It's just because you've been away for so long. You know he loves you. He's just nervous. He wouldn't throw everything we have away.* Against my own intuition, I acquiesced. But honestly, I no longer felt the security that I once felt in our relationship. My peace was gone. I *knew* something wasn't right; I just didn't know the the full extent of the wrong.

Note: Ladies, let me talk specifically to you about this because I'm coming from a woman's perspective. I could probably write a whole other book on this subject, but I'll do my best to keep it brief. I don't claim to be an expert in this area—this is my opinion based on my experience. Naturally this does not apply to every woman, but I feel that once a woman puts "real" energy, effort, and time into a man, *and* gives her body to him, she views that relationship as more than just casual dating. She's made the decision to give that man the core essence of who she is—the part of her that is precious and sacred. So metaphorically, she has begun "investing" in her future and as with any investment, hopes to yield a profit. I'm specifically referring to a period of time in a monogamous relationship that a woman has with a man. A relationship where a couple has been dating for a while. They've "discussed" marriage and joint future goals. Because of that, that woman usually does *all* the things married people do, although she is not yet his wife. There is an unspoken "contract of understanding" that exists, where the terms are not written, but executed. She plays a role, (he does too), in expectation that the pay off will be worth the investment. I am confident that many women have played this role before to no avail.

Now, let me state the obvious: BIG MISTAKE!!! And the reasons are plentiful! I already mentioned the spiritual ramifications of sex outside of marriage in chapter 4, so here let's just talk freely. This does not apply to every woman, but I most certainly think there are many to whom it does. From a natural standpoint, if you really think about it ladies, we're the ones walking the tightrope. Ever heard the phrase, "Why buy the milk when the cow is free?" This phrase is a no-brainer! Yet it is too often the pitfall for us when it comes to relationships. Once a woman thinks her future is secure and "locks" in to a man, she willfully succumbs to the wife role, believing it is just a matter of time before she is actually his wife. She imagines her wedding day, (maybe children), and all the plans that bring her closer to her dream. Her faith and trust are in *him*. Essentially, she has put all her "eggs in one basket."

Then…the bottom falls out, and she's left wondering how it happened when she did everything! If this sounds at all familiar, "all men are *not* dogs." However, "if you lie with dogs, you will most certainly get up with fleas." What I'm trying to bring to your attention here is that we, women, put ourselves in that position. Whether out of desperation, personal/outside pressure, or even good intentions, *WE* set ourselves up! I know you may not like it, don't want to hear it, or believe it, but it is a harsh reality. Even though we are excellent multitaskers, and can bear great pressure, we are primarily emotional beings. We think, act, and move on our emotions. We like purses, shoes, jewelry—all these things make us feel *outwardly* beautiful. But if our man fixed a homemade candlelight dinner and put on a show for us, or if he ran a warm bath with rose petals and massaged us with the nice aromatic oils, or if he truly engaged in deep conversation about our concerns, with interest, our heartstrings would play a symphony, because it is very intimate to us *emotionally*.

These "loving" gestures are usually early in a relationship. So the tiniest prospect of those inward desires being fulfilled, causes a full-speed-ahead plunge without much hesitation from us. We see potential in him and we have desire for him, so we invest deeper. We are *mentally* stronger in our commitment to him, and *choose* to trust in the relationship. We move faster than we should, trying to get to the "happily ever after" before the main event (the wedding) ever takes place. We never consider any other scenario because our minds have already played out our story and we've convinced ourselves "this is right." We compromise and sacrifice to get there, overlooking things we think can be "sorted out later."

Ladies, the ugly truth is, it's *our* fault! Yes, we can blame *him* for all the terrible things he said and did with validity and truth, but it doesn't excuse our own culpability. A person, be it man or woman, can only do what you allow him/her to do to you. So did you accept his disrespect toward you? Any mistreatment or abuse? Were you uncomfortable, insecure, or suspicious? Did you soul search as to why you suddenly felt differently in the relationship? Did you *do* anything? *Say* anything? Certainly, you didn't feel this way when you first started dating or your relationship would have never have made it that far. Think back…what was the first thing you *allowed*? (Especially if you discussed or fought about it with him). *WHY* did you overlook it? Was it a big deal to you? And what was *his* response? Was it nonchalant? Did he say it was silly? Ridiculous? Why exactly, did you accept that?

I say it's because of all that time you invested—all those compromises and sacrifices you made. Now you don't have the luxury of giving up, giving in, or giving out. You've come too far, put in too much time. It has to work! What will people say? Were you "warned" by anyone? You think, *if I just hang it there, I can change that.* But what you really mean is, you think you can change *him*. How honest can you be with yourself? It's difficult and painful, I know. But I believe that deep down, we already knew the answers to the questions that plagued us—they were just not what we wanted to admit. Maya Angelou said, "When a person shows you who they are, believe them the first time."

So, think back. Was there *any* indication at all? What did you *do* about it then? If you answered, "yes" or "not much," therein lies your culpability. Even if you expressed "disapproval" but *stayed*, it's still on you.

Beautiful Woman, do you know who you are? You belong to God! You were made to be a helpmeet and a blessing to a man. You are on loan from God to him, but *only* if he proves himself worthy. You are God's creation; made in His image and His likeness, and blessed by Him (Genesis 1:26-28). You have meaning, purpose, and value! It doesn't matter what you look like, what you own, or what you have or haven't accomplished. You are precious in God's eyes and He loves you unconditionally! That means even with your faults and shortcomings, you are still His favorite! About the investment you made in that man, Jesus made a much greater one on the Cross for you! Don't be fooled, there is *no* man on Earth that can love you like this! Man's love is conditional and moody, changing from day to day. And you are jumping through hoops regularly, trying to figure out how to get it right and keep him pleased. You can never live up to someone else's expectations. Truth is, you can't even live up to your own! How many times have you disappointed yourself? Second guessed or failed yourself? Yet, you think you can keep someone else happy? Wake up!

That is not your role.

Woman of God, you are a precious and rare gem in this world! You are loved by the greatest One that ever lived! *You are only complete in Him.* Learn to love yourself first, with all your flaws and imperfections, only then can you truly love someone else. Believe in yourself. Trust yourself. Accept the fact that you've got issues, yet are cherished by the Creator and Master of the entire universe!

Establish boundaries and standards to date by; to live by; and don't change them to please anyone but Him. Make up your mind that you won't settle for less just so you're not alone. You deserve better and God has better for you. Doing the same things will yield the same results. If you keep filling that space with Mr. Wrong, you will never see the Mr. Right God has coming.

So you ask, "How will you know Mr. Right?" **Most importantly, Mr. Right loves God with all his heart, mind, soul, and strength, and puts Him first.** A man that loves the Lord *like this* will seek God on how to love you, because he wants to please the Father. He understands that you are both works in progress, but that two are still better together. He should want to bring out the best in you because you are his gift from God. You should be able to glean from him and mature in your walk because of *his* relationship with the Lord. He covers you and cares for you. You should be a better woman because of him, not a bitter one. You should feel stronger with him than alone, and together strive for the greatness God has ordained for your union.

You will never be who God designed you to be if you're always with the wrong man. Stop your own looking and wait on God. HE knows *what* is best for you and *who* is best for you too. The Bible says in Proverbs 18:22 (ESV), that he who finds a wife finds a good thing and obtains favor from the Lord. So take a breath. Calm down. Be patient and wait on the Lord. Give Mr. Right a chance to find you! He is made in God's image as well, with purpose and meaning to his life. His seeking God will reveal that and lead him to you, through God's will. You also have to be ready, so you don't ruin God's gift to you. Then the two of you can walk out that vision together as one. Amos 3:3 asks, "Can two walk together, except they be agreed?" And Psalm 37:23 states, "The steps of a good man are ordered by the Lord..."

A man can't possibly lead if he doesn't know who he is or where he's going, so there is no benefit or blessing for you there. And if *you're* running things, you're already out of order. I say wait on the Lord, who is able to fulfill *all* your heart's desires. Wait, I say, on the Lord.

 Establish boundaries and standards to date by; to live by; and don't change them to please anyone but Him.

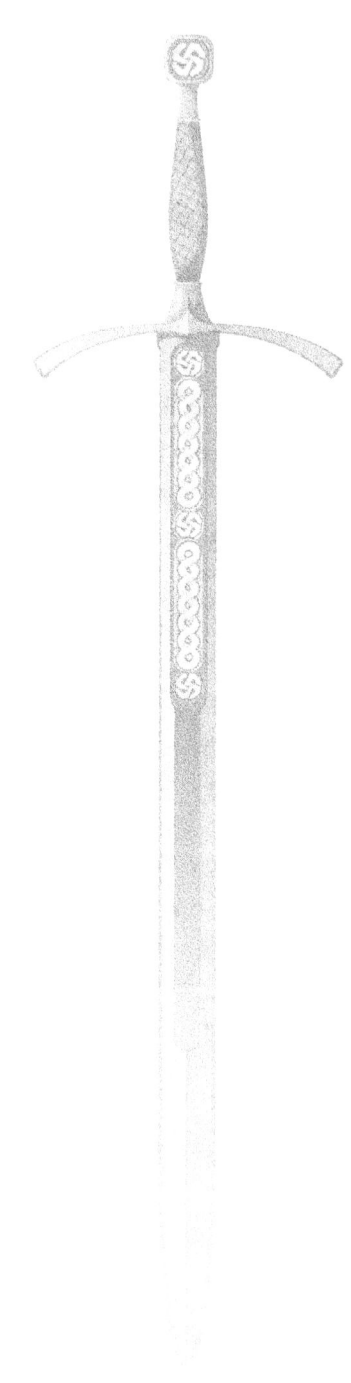

CONFLICTED
The Battle Within

About a week later, my good friend G, drove me, my cat (Smokey), and the rest of my belongings to the airport. There was so much on my mind. I was sad when I should have been happy. My thoughts were all over the place but I tried to play it off to the best of my ability. G's not one to pry so she never asked, but I knew she knew something was wrong. She had been one of my best friends for twenty years! We should have been celebrating and reminiscing on our own good times, but I was too troubled and concerned about what I was heading towards. I tried to keep things light so I wouldn't fall apart in the car, but once I was alone at the gate, my emotions overwhelmed me. I felt numb as I was almost last to board the plane. I took my window seat and stared blankly outside seeing nothing, but inwardly, in chaotic turmoil. As the plane began to back out the gate, my tears began to flow. I wondered what would have happened if I had shouted, "Wait, stop! I need to get off!" I'll never know because I didn't do it. By the time the plane began to ascend into the air, I was crying almost uncontrollably. The passenger next to me couldn't help but to say something. She first thought I was afraid of flying. Then she thought I had lost a loved one. I could feel her compassion and sympathy for me. (She was partly right though, I had lost someone—myself). I did my best to front. I thanked her and told her I'd be OK and just kept my face towards the window. The sweet stewardesses also came to see if they could help me, but no one could help. I sobbed the entire duration of the flight. By the time we arrived and people started to deplane, it felt like everyone was walking by trying to get a glimpse of *the poor girl by the window*. I must have looked pitiful. I kept my face hidden and my head down pretending to attend to my cat while I waited to be almost last off the plane. The stewardesses were all standing by the door then, with tenderness and compassion in their eyes, not knowing what to say. I managed a 'thank you' as I walked by, feeling like I had been in a physical fight. I headed straight to the restroom to try to freshen up a bit because I was about to be picked up by a total stranger. For whatever reason, I didn't want this man to see me for the first time looking like a train wreck. I don't remember his name but I know he was Bae's next door neighbor. He tried to make small talk on the way back but I could only manage short direct answers. My insides were screaming so loudly that I thought he might hear them if my mouth was open too long. When we arrived at the complex, he took my bags, led me to Bae's door, handed me the key, and graciously extended his or his wife's help, should I need anything while Bae was away. I thanked him and quickly opened the door because I was anxious to be alone. I'm sure he noticed I was desperately fighting back tears.

Once inside, I put the pet carrier down, leaned up against the back of the door and let the tears flow. I couldn't shake the sinking feeling that I was in trouble. Not sure how long I was there, the meows from my cat eventually brought me back to the present. I unzipped the carrier to let him out. After a brief cuddle, we both began to examine our new surroundings.

The condo was nice, relatively spacious. As I crossed the doorway's threshold, I was standing next to the outer wall of the master bedroom on my right, and the hall closet on my left. The dining area was a few steps ahead on the left, and shared a common wall with the closet. There was a staircase along the left wall leading down to the garage, where the washer and dryer were located. The kitchen entry was across from the dining area. On the right side of that entry, was a marble countertop that curved around like a bar, where two could sit and have a quick meal. To the right of that, was a familiar armchair sitting in the space against the wall. Crossing a hallway on the other side of the room, was the living room, with the armchair's matching furniture, though I saw a new coffee table and TV for the first time. The sofa sat against the shared wall on the outside of the master bedroom, and the love seat made an L shape, parallel with the hallway's path. There was a nice balcony that ran the length of the living room, but its view only overlooked the parking lot.

The second bedroom was about ten feet down the hallway towards the back. The room had a queen size bed in it with a matching dresser. The closet was a good size, and the bathroom was located inside the room. After a quick look, that is where I took my luggage & belongings. I wasn't particularly feeling comfortable or welcome.

There was no fanfare when I walked in; no banners or streamers hanging, not even a loving message or note that expressed any joy or excitement of my coming. It felt flat and uninviting, like I was imposing. I didn't want to unpack, I wanted to run. I felt edgy and uncertain. I sat on the bed and cried again. Sick of myself, I sighed remorsefully, trying to accept an undeniable mistake.

Eventually, I willed myself up and looked around. I started in his room, the cabinets, the closets, the bathrooms, the refrigerator, and the garage. It all appeared fine at first, but something didn't *feel* right. I felt compelled to look deeper. I didn't know what I was exactly searching for, but I knew in my gut that I would know it when I saw it. I searched through those same places again and my eyes began to see things I overlooked before. First, I saw a different brand of coffee in the cupboard and a different brand of turkey bacon in the refrigerator. We had been together a few years and we always bought one brand of coffee. We didn't drink instant, yet there was a jar of a different brand in the cabinet. That particular brand of turkey bacon in the refrigerator, would *never* be in the house! Bae was adamant about that. So I am looking at not one, but two "major" items that *he* would never buy! *I knew then it was a Rookie's mistake.* My senses were heightened now and I felt a nervous rush of adrenaline. I went into his room. I looked in the drawers, the nightstands, the closet. Everything seemed normal. I mostly saw the things I had given him over the years – cards, knickknacks, clothes. Then, I went to his bathroom. That is where my heart dropped. Under the sink in the cabinet, was a bottle of contact solution…*but we both wore glasses!*

    Stop. Now you may think I was overreacting or perhaps deserved what I got because I was "looking." You're very welcome to that opinion. But real talk, it's *my* opinion that many women do this same thing. We're natural "detectives;" and detectives, detect! They look for small signs and/or clues that the average person would overlook or not even know to look for. We investigate especially when our intuition is heightened.

    In my defense, we had *always* shared everything. We knew each other's pin numbers and codes; we answered each other's phones and signed each other's names on things. This relocation uprooted my entire life; a decision *we* had discussed and made together. My engagement ring was *supposedly* being sized, and we were *planning* to marry within the next year. We were *supposed* to start house hunting and begin our new life together as one. Keep in mind this plan was in motion before *he* left Cali over a year ago. So, I feel I had a right to do exactly what I was doing. He should have even expected it.

    At that moment, I felt sick in my stomach, I probably even gasped aloud. I was horrified! I could feel my mind replaying everything in slow motion, as I began to connect the dots: his change in behavior, our miscommunications, the awkward silences, his "disappearances." The very thing I never wanted to entertain, I now knew in my knower. Not only was he cheating, but playing house with another woman! A gamut of emotions hit me all at once making me dizzy. My legs were weak so I slid down against the bathroom wall in shock. The moments afterward were surreal. I wondered if my mind was playing tricks on me—were my eyes actually seeing correctly? Was I awake or dreaming? My mind was blown. I couldn't do anything but cry.

> *The very thing I never wanted to entertain,*

My only companion at that moment came to check on me. Smokey came and rubbed up against me with an arched back, circling and purring for attention the way cats do. I instinctively reached out to pet him but even he knew my heart wasn't in it. Eventually he just curled up against me and laid down, still purring. My mind continued to replay different scenes in my head. I don't know how long I sat there in utter turmoil and confusion. I was devastated. I had trouble believing it. I was at a loss of what to do because I couldn't think straight. I loved him and hated him, then loved him and hated him again, over and over. I kept trying to figure out what had happened. Did *I* do something wrong? Was this *my* fault? Why would he be so careless and stupid? Wait, was this on purpose? The more I thought, the madder I got. It was *not* my fault! And this needed to be dealt with immediately, but I still had to wait another two days for his return.

 *Keep me safe from the traps set by evildoers,
from the snares they have laid for me.*

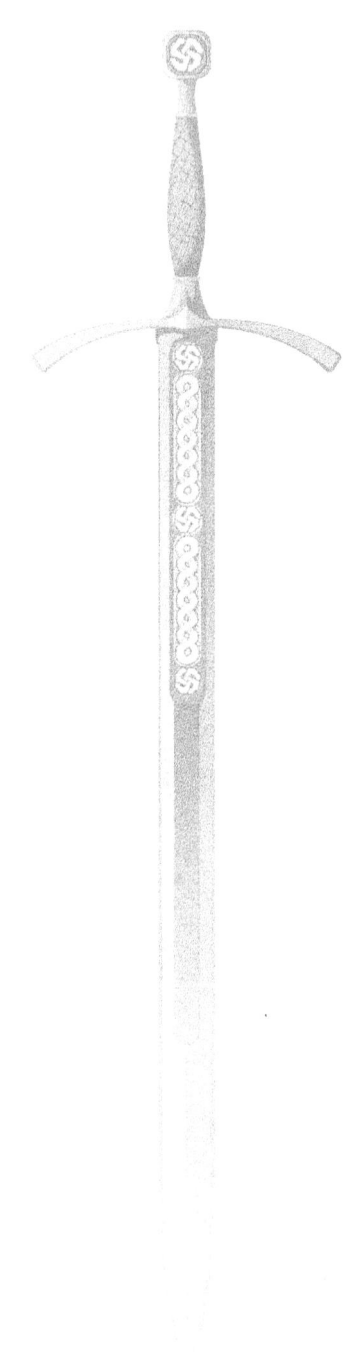

BEHIND ENEMY LINES
Waging War

I had barely slept or eaten. My nerves were frazzled and my head ached from thinking so much…but Saturday had arrived! I was full of mixed emotions, while anger and anxiety held the top spots. I had rehearsed and replayed dozens of conversations over and over in my head. I had anticipated every possible scenario and response. There was nothing left for me to do except confront him about it all. I waited quite impatiently for his arrival, the way a caged animal restlessly paces back and forth. The longer it took for him to return, the more restless I became. My mind invented all sorts of stories.

By the time the car pulled up in front of the building, I literally felt like I would pop! I kept trying to calm myself down because I knew his daughters were back too. I needed to exercise some restraint, so I was trying to bring myself down from the roof to at least the ceiling. I'm a no-nonsense type of person, so this was very hard for me. I was supposed to be "the welcome home party" for the girls now, but I felt more like a Mack truck revving its engine, the way a race car does before the light turns green! Finally, the key turned in the door. The girls rushed in first, excited to see me. I greeted them with hugs and kisses under a big smile, professing how much I had missed them. Bae on the other hand, only *acted* happy to see me. He gave me a peck and a fake hug, (at least that was my thought). I was inwardly already filled with disdain and contempt. For the time being I bit my tongue, for the sake of the girls. Honestly, I was ready for the bell to sound and the first round to begin. I knew there would be a fight, but I was ready! Instead, I began with the niceties, and casual conversation. I asked general questions about the trip, pretending to be interested, but secretly gritting my teeth with every idle word.

I learned something about myself a long time ago: that if I have to bite my tongue too long about something, or if I don't get to express myself and release that mounting stress within me, I get physically nauseous! I'm direct and outspoken. And since I had been holding this in for days, it was literally making me sick.

Time seemed as if it was almost standing still. I was feeling sharp pains in my stomach, (*more like abrupt stabbing sensations)*. Several of them made me grab my stomach secretly and wince. Controlling myself till the girls' bedtime was arduous. It was a real labor of love because I wanted to be selfish like I felt he was. I wanted not to care, but they would have been collateral damage.

Alas, my time had arrived! The girls were fast asleep, and the two of us were alone together. I decided to start out *easy* so he wouldn't get defensive right away— to kind of feel him out. For me, that means asking questions that I already know the answers to but play dumb about. I consider it a "love tap" in the boxing ring. It affords the other person the opportunity to easily tell the truth because it's a "non-threatening" question. Therefore, that first answer is usually a telltale sign of who you'll be dealing with. (A lie on a love tap, means big trouble!)

Bae had told me more than once that he would rather eat pork bacon than to eat *that* brand in the fridge, so I asked about the bacon first. I gave some excuse about fixing my breakfast and discovering *that* bacon. He responded that there was no more of the brand *we* liked in the store. (LIE! Red flag!) What an unbelievable answer! Nevertheless it wasn't impossible, so I countered by asking why he hadn't gotten the "alternative brand" he liked in its stead. I received the same poor answer, with the added excuse that that particular store didn't have much of anything.

From your perspective, you may not see anything wrong here, but I knew him. I thought *ok, here we go*. So after that, it went something like this:

"Really? What kind of store was this? *One* brand of bacon? And what about the instant coffee? Why is that here?"

"Oh, I just grabbed the first thing I saw because I was in a hurry that day." (My mind was reeling... *the audacity!*)

I said, "That much of a hurry that you'd buy an instant coffee that you don't drink *and* it's decaf? What kind of store was this again? Where were you?"

I can't say for sure what he was thinking, but I knew he knew that I knew he was lying. He started moving around uncomfortably, trying to look busy while avoiding eye contact. I, on the other hand, was already angry. Angry because he chose to lie to me. Obviously he was cheating! But most importantly because he was insulting my intelligence! So, I threw my first punch!

"Ok. And why is there contact solution in the bathroom when you don't wear contacts?!" It was a straight uppercut to the chin, and he felt it. He had no response because he knew he wasn't fast enough on the draw for that, so he shut down.

"What's with all the questions?! Man, I just got home. I'm tired and want to relax."

"Relax? You tell me then, what's with all the lies? Do you need to tell me something? Are you cheating?..Because you're obviously lying!"

"I'm not gonna talk about this right now."

"Talk about what? What is '*this?*' Do you mean your cheating? Or your lying?"

No answer. He turned on the TV. Ticked off to the nth degree, I said, "Uh, hello?"

"I'm not gonna argue with you."

"The only reason we're gonna argue is because you're not talking! This can be resolved right now, but you *do* need to talk to me."

Silence.

I was not to be trifled with! He was not going to have his way! The realization that I couldn't go on the cruise because *she* probably went, stung. He could have gone by himself with the girls, but he most likely didn't. As things began to unfold in my mind, I let it all come out so I wouldn't have any stomach pains. He probably would have loved for me to shut up, but that *was not* gonna happen! My monologue began.

"So you're really gonna sit there and not say anything? Why are you quiet now? The lies were flowing so easily before, what happened? Cat got your tongue? Did I throw you off guard with the contact solution? Oh, you didn't know she left that, or did you just not care? The least you could have done was make sure the place was *clean* before I arrived! I didn't come all this way for some bullsh*t? So tell me, what's the story here? How long has this actually been going on? Are you in love with her? Because you're obviously *not* in love with me! People in love don't do things like this! So what's up? Tell me what I need to know!"

Silence.

"You're not gonna say anything? Really? You owe me nothing? Answer me!"

He said nothing. I turned and went into my room, got my phone, and walked out the front door.

I had no idea where I was going. I hadn't been out of the place since I arrived. It was dark out and I had absolutely no idea of my surroundings. I remember running down the stairs and finding my way out onto the street. It was close to 11pm and it began raining. I called my Mom but it took a moment for her to get to the phone. I realized I was choking on the huge lump that was in my throat. Hearing her voice allowed the floodgates to open. I burst into tears and said, "Mom, he doesn't want me anymore." I was full out sobbing now, similar to that on the plane, but this time, I didn't have to hold anything in. I just kept repeating, "He doesn't want me anymore." My sweet Mom tried to calm me down and assess the situation at the same time. It must have been awful for her too. I heard her speaking to someone saying something like 'she wasn't sure what was happening and that she was trying to understand. She let me cry, but called my name a few times with that gentle soothing voice, to see if I was calm enough to speak. I estimate about five minutes had gone by before she was able to get through to me. Wanting to know what had happened, I told her everything.

My Mom is one of the sweetest, kindest people I've ever known. She's beautiful and gentle, yet extremely strong. She's compassionate and generous; slow to anger or judge, and quick to forgive. She's an excellent listener and full of wisdom. She's the kind that will "take the blow" so that you're unscathed.

She gently asked my location and if I was in danger. Then she wanted to know where *he* was. She was concerned because of the late hour and that I was in the rain. She told me to try to find my way back and that she would stay on the phone with me. But I didn't want to go back! As a mother, I can only imagine what she was going through that night. She was too far away to get to me. Her daughter was alone and hysterical, in a new state where neither of us knew anybody. She had no one to call to "rescue" her *Baby*. The one person she had entrusted her daughter to, now seemed to be the one that couldn't be trusted. I'm sure she was somewhat disturbed and confused, but it was important for her to remain calm while I was in my current state. She did her best to convince me to try to return but she couldn't, (I really didn't know where I was). Then she asked me what I wanted to do. For some reason, that question caught me off guard. I quieted down because several things hit my mind all at once. I hadn't thought about anything past that moment but now I had to. It seemed that should have been an easy question to answer, but the more I thought about it, the more confused I became. *I hated him and loved him.*

Maybe instinctively, I responded that I didn't know, but asked if she could call one of my brother's and have him call me. No sooner had I said that, Bae pulled up in front of me in the car. He opened the door for me to get in but I was reluctant. He never said anything but saw I was on the phone. I stood there telling my Mom everything as the events unfolded. She told me that he had probably been looking for me and that I should get in the car, but I didn't want to. My disdain for him was off the charts and the very sight of him angered me. My Mom asked about my safety again. Once I responded that I wasn't in any danger, she kept trying to convince me to go back with him so I wouldn't get sick. I could care less about being sick! I didn't want to move. Finally she told me that she wouldn't call my brother until she knew I was back in the house and out of the rain. That got me because I *really* wanted to talk to my brother above everything else.

I'm the seventh of nine children. All of my older brothers and sisters are "stair steps" in age. This brother is the one above me, although there is a six year gap between us. He's not a huge guy at all; about 6', maybe 6"1', no more than about 150 pounds on his best day soaking wet. But he was smart, fast, and dangerous. At that time, he worked for one of the Government's top agencies. He was "on assignment" most of the time and very hard to get in touch with because of his duties and responsibilities. He purposely kept a distance from the family and communication rare, because of his line of work. But if he ever came on the scene, he meant business and was not to be taken lightly. *He* was the brother I was looking for. *He* was the one I wanted to reach. Why? The reckoning!

I got in the car but kept my Mom on the line. The tension was extremely thick and he didn't say one word. It turned out we weren't far from his place, but I wouldn't have known how to get there. I had run out blindly and continued walking aimlessly in the rain while talking to my Mom. I was last to get out of the car, last to come up the steps, last to enter back into the house. I told my Mom step by step what I was doing. I wasn't afraid but I should have learned from Ex that it served me best to have a plan in every situation. Yet I didn't have one. For now, I could only relay my immediate steps to my Mom on the phone. I entered the house, went straight to *my* room and closed the door. I stayed on the line with my Mom because it kept my mind occupied, and I was somewhat comforted. She was back to the question of what I wanted to do when I heard a light knock on the door.

"What!" I snapped.

He opened the door and asked if we could talk.

"About what?" I responded while still on the phone,

allowing my Mom to hear what was going on.

My mother asked to speak to him so I stretched out my arm towards him with phone in hand. He hesitated, then took it and put it to his ear saying, "hello." I don't know what my Mom said to him but his response was that he loved me but we had to work out a few things. She then said something else that he said "ok" to, then reached out to hand the phone back to me. Hearing my voice, she went on to tell me to talk with him and see if we could work things out. She made the promise of being available should I need her, that she loved me, and that I could always call her back if necessary. With that, I reluctantly hung up the phone. I couldn't look at him immediately because I was disgusted at the sight of him. I sat there on the edge of the bed waiting for him to start talking.

Stop. Now let me interject something here for a minute that I feel is important. I told you earlier that I am outspoken and direct. I am also highly analytical, opinionated, and easily excitable. I'm a "fighter" by nature, and not easily swayed. I dig and look for the root or "truth" of the problem, so you can't just brush over things easily with me. I listen to words. So depending on the words used, I might interpret what someone says in a different way than what is actually meant. I've been criticized and accused repeatedly of being "too literal" and/or "analytical." Growing up, I wanted to be a lawyer or a psychologist. I became neither but often hear from others that they understand why I should have been. I'll be the first to admit my edges are rough. One thing was sure, the same power and passion I loved you with, is the same power and passion you'd feel if we were at odds with each other. In my past relationships, people (especially men) dismissed that warning with a chuckle, only to witness it later when I was their "adversary." This is where Bae now found himself.

I sat somewhat anxiously waiting for him to say something. It took him a minute, I figured he did not know how to start. To be honest, I don't even recall the conversation. Why? Two big reasons! First, it didn't start with an apology of *any* kind for *any* thing, and secondly, because he *never* admitted his wrongdoing. Because of that, everything that came out of his mouth was meaningless to me; it was a total waste of my time!

My phone rang in the midst. *Who could be calling me at this hour?* It was my brother! I could hardly believe it myself because I couldn't remember the last time we actually spoke. I was elated! I answered by saying his name aloud so Bae would know. My one-sided conversation sounded something like this to him, 'that I was ok'; 'no, he hadn't touched me'; 'that I didn't think so' (that I was in danger); and that 'we were talking when he called'. I went on to say that I would keep him informed and let him know when/if I needed him to come. I then said, "Goodbye," and thanked him for checking on me, and being there for me. I hung up with a new sense of strength and pride. There was new air in my lungs! But Bae was taken aback. Shock and disbelief on his face.

He said, "You called *your* brother?" He may not have been phased by anyone else I spoke to, but he knew about my brother!

Looking at him, I huffed with confidence, "Yea, what about it?"

"I can't believe you called your brother."

"Why not? I may need his help."

Bae just shook his head, mumbling about the fact that I called my brother. I felt he should have been nominated for an Oscar, because he knew he was heading for round two of a fight he couldn't win. Using it as an excuse to duck and run, that's exactly what he did. He turned around and walked out the door shaking his head.

I said, "Oh, so now you don't wanna talk anymore? You're that shocked? Really? That's your best excuse? Guess you'll use anything to keep your lie covered…whatever. Humph."

I don't know for sure what he did after that but I have my suspicions. I got up, slammed the door shut, and locked it. Behind that closed door, I let my guard down. I was already beating myself up for being stupid after being forewarned a year ago. I again, recounted all the question marks that had grabbed my attention along the way but remained ignored. The self- condemnation was merciless!

Emotionally drained, I finally fell asleep. I awoke the next morning feeling out of sorts, wondering if I had been dreaming. Scanning my surroundings quickly reminded me of the nightmare I was currently living. I don't remember what time it was, but I heard little voices talking in the other room eagerly wanting to awaken me. He told them that I was probably exhausted, so to let me rest a bit longer. I scoffed and rolled my eyes. I was in no hurry to see anyone, (especially him), but figured I should surface in another hour or so. Still angry, I did my best not to look at or say much to him. I was on a real tightrope, but had purposed in my mind to "be nice" as long as the girls were there.

The group Earth, Wind, and Fire, sang a song about the 'twelfth of never'. That's how long I felt like I was biting my tongue! Every day was more agonizing than the day before. I truly cannot have things fester inside. The longer I held it in, the stronger my regret, anger, and resentment grew. I kept a headache and my stomach stayed upset.

There were no more confrontations while the girls were there. We each played our respective roles and sidelined any conflicts for their sake. I kept asking myself why I should care if they heard anything, but my moral conscience disallowed all backlash. They were innocent in this fight, and I couldn't willingly hurt them.

Once the girls left, we remained "cordial" in our relationship, but that wasn't working for me. Without conversation, we were both walking on egg shells. I needed to talk, hash things out. But he was perfectly content to skirt the issue. *The nerve!* He had ample "down" time while the girls were with us, to figure out an approach. We needed to have an adult conversation, but the more he ran, the deeper the hole got. I know he knew there was no easy way out, especially having to deal with my attitude. The same way I'm sure he was running around being "The Man" before I arrived, I wanted him to "man up" now and face *me!* Of course, he didn't.

I hated having to depend on him for anything, but neither the moving truck nor my car had arrived yet. I loathed him. I talked to my Mom everyday to keep her abreast of my situation. He didn't know it, but I had "called off" my brother.

A week later, my belongings arrived. I'm sure we were both relieved. Time was passing and we still hadn't talked things out. It was obvious the relationship was over, but not talking wasn't a good sign. I knew I had made that terrible mistake a second time, (long distance love), and I was furious about it! I meditated constantly on everything I had done for him in the past two and a half years versus how I was now being treated. It didn't sit well, and I was angered by it. That passionate love I once had for him was flipping with the same intensity. There was no kindling of love within me at the moment, but a raging fire of resentment and animosity. My breathing changed at the sight of him and my heart rate and blood pressure increased. If my eyes could shoot darts, every inch of him would have been pierced. The words I did speak were cold and abrupt. The intensity of my rage grew rapidly and was getting harder to conceal or contain. I wished we could have talked things through, and reached some kind of understanding or agreement - perhaps some of that contempt would have subsided. Not because I wouldn't have been angry, but I would have considered it a sign of respect towards me, however menial. But that *never* happened. And by November, he had moved out and in with his new Girl.

 When we don't honor God the way we should, we fall into traps and pitfalls repeatedly.

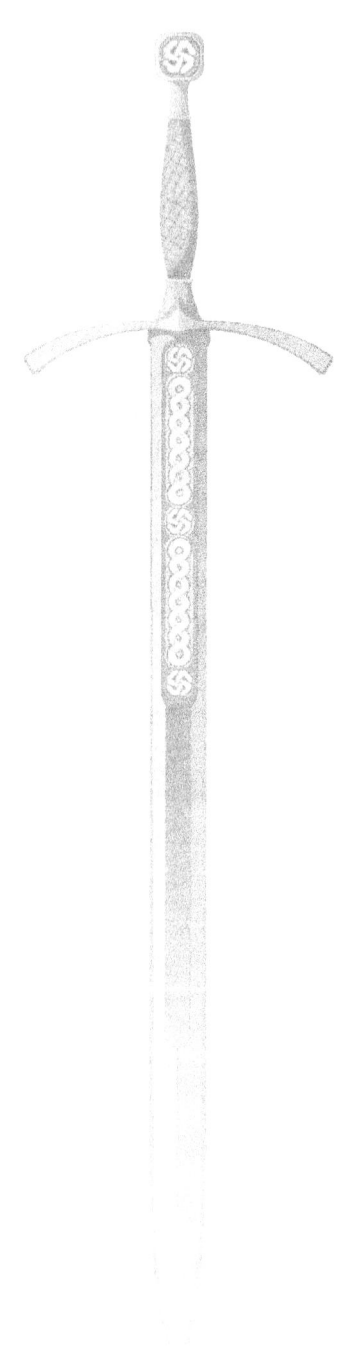

GOD IN THE MIDST
His Saving Grace

Try not to judge me too harshly here. I'm giving you real talk about me—*my* attitude and *my* behavior. I did a lot wrong, but I was terribly wronged as well. I was then, and still am, a work in progress.

I titled this chapter *God in the Midst* because I discovered this truth long after this season passed. I did not realize it when I was going through because my rage had blinded me. But like the prodigal son, in Luke 15:17, when I came to myself, meaning, when my *right* mind returned and I was able to think clearly, I saw God's hand had always protected me, especially in my darkest times. James 1:20

(AMP) states, "For the (resentful, deep-seated) anger of man does not produce the righteousness of God (that standard of behavior which He requires from us)." My mind had been consumed with anger, resentment, and unforgiveness; all of which are *not* God-like characteristics. Oh, the love of God is phenomenal; truly impossible to understand. It surpasses all human knowledge and comprehension, and is beyond what we could possibly think or imagine. When God says that He is for you, (Romans 8:31), that He goes before you and will be with you; that He'll never leave you nor forsake you, (Deuteronomy 31:8), He means it! Joy unspeakable comes when *you learn* to believe Him (1 Peter 1:8)! This chapter contains a few of the examples where I later realized how protected I was by that Love, and how God covered me with His Grace and Mercy. Amen.

Between those couple months from August to November, much had happened. Bae and I *shared* the condo somewhat peacefully, but only because he was rarely there. We had little to no contact, and communicated only when necessary, usually by text or email. We had our own routines and rarely crossed paths. He would come "home" every Tuesday while I was at work, to check on things, pick up his mail, or get clothes. Occasionally, there would be something out of place in the house, or something insignificant on the counter that announced his visit. I didn't care until I noticed kitchen items started disappearing. (All my belongings were in storage, which meant I would either have to go buy that item or do without). It would have been more acceptable with a heads-up first, but I didn't like the sneaky way it was being done – no note, no warning, and of course while I'm not home! It enraged me every time I went to use something and it was gone, especially considering how much I had done for him when he first moved there! *Just make sure you don't touch any of **my** stuff or there's gonna be trouble!* But God had it that whatever I *felt* I needed, He in some way, provided.

Now, I'm not the neatest person in the world but I am meticulous about many things. Have you ever put something somewhere in a particular place or order, then gone back to find it's not like you had it? Not an obvious change, but noticeable to *you,* that something is a little off. It's a subtle difference; one that might cause you to think twice for a moment. You may wonder *if* you actually left it that way. (Ok, so I'm that kind of thinker. I have the kind of mind that works overtime, even on a simple thing—needing to understand the *why* of a thing). I will think, *"It wouldn't make sense for me to do that, so why did I?"* My own mind often gave me headaches from thinking so much, especially in this period of my life. I stayed on high alert and everything was scrutinized. I'd have restless and sleepless nights if I latched on to something puzzling. It would consume my mind until I felt I had a reasonable explanation. Even then, it would have to fall in line with *my* way of thinking and doing things before I could accept it.

Now there were times I'd come home from work and find my things slightly out of place in my room. The first time, I didn't think much of it. It was something small, I think a greeting card was in a different spot or facing a different way. I noticed, but chalked it up to distress and fatigue. *I don't know, maybe I did leave it like that and don't remember.*

Another time, I noticed my papers were out of order. For example, instead of being 1,2,3,4,5, they were 1,2,4,3,5, or something like that. *Well, I was looking at them the other day...maybe I left them like that.* I'd be curious, maybe even a tad suspicious, but I thought it *possible* in my current state of mind. But a third time, something amiss in *my* room? Absolutely not! My obsession began. I went back and rethought about the first time with the card. I forced myself to trace every step. It was quite challenging because everything else in my room, and the house, would look the same way it had when I went to work. Bae still had his keys and could come and go as he pleased, so I began to question why he would go through my things. *Why was he meddling in my stuff? Was he being nosy or jealous? I'll have to see...*

Before I relocated, I had accepted that bid on my house in Cali. It was to bring me a large profit, but I was still waiting for the paperwork to finalize. Things moved slower than usual because the market was shifting then and the Holidays were quickly approaching. I was worried I wouldn't finalize till February or March of the following year. Honestly, I didn't want things dragging out till then. I knew Bae didn't either. He kept pestering me, asking questions about it. He paid for the rent and bills in Florida while I paid for my mortgage and bills in Cali. That was our agreement before the move, and so stood now. I hurriedly let him know that I had no desire to stay where I wasn't wanted and that when I knew something, he'd know something. Till then, stop bugging me! He didn't have to worry, living there everyday was a constant reminder of my plight and pain and I desperately wanted out! I could hardly stand him!

One day, I was off from work. I was grateful not to have to make that hour drive and struggle through hours of hidden unhappiness and tears. I was enjoying my time at home with Smokey. He had been a real lifesaver for me because he infiltrated the barrier of loneliness and being alone. He loved me with unabated affection and always made me feel better.

I needed to check my emails for any news. The computer was in Bae's room close to the front door. I'd use it regularly to communicate with Bae, my realtor, or friends from Cali. I had just logged off the computer and was about two steps out of Bae's room when I heard the key in the door. Smokey ran towards the door to greet him. I ran to my room and went into the bathroom, because I wasn't ready to see or deal with him. I turned on the faucet in the sink and washed my hands, pretending to have used the bathroom. Then I waited an additional few moments before going out so I could gather myself in preparation of whatever was coming. When I walked out into the common area, there was no one there. The junk mail was on top of the wall by the stairs so I knew he had come into the house, but I didn't hear or see him. I looked down the stairs towards the garage, but the door was still closed. I walked toward his room and called his name, but he didn't answer. There was no sign of him. Confused, I looked around for a minute. I knew I heard the key in the lock, the cat had confirmed that by running to the door. There was mail sitting inside which hadn't been there before, yet no one was in the house. Then it hit me! I tore through the front door and ran down the stairs to the parking lot. My eyes scanned everywhere. I was looking for *anything* moving! I don't know how long I stayed there looking and waiting, but I can tell you it was the Grace of God that I didn't search car to car! Heat was coming from my entire body! I finally made my way back inside still looking with expectation, but to no avail. Suspicious, I turned on the radio and soon heard Bae's voice. He was doing a show in Orlando. It wasn't him that came to the house, it was *her*! Obviously she knew I wasn't normally home during that time, but she didn't know I had taken the day off, and he was out of town. How dare she use his key to enter *my* space! Immediately, I understood why my things were misplaced. *She* was the one that had been nosing around in my stuff! I remember thinking, *Yeah, you better run! If you really want to meet me, I'm right here!*

    I'm telling you about it, but only God truly knows the rage that bubbled inside me. It was His Grace that prevented that encounter. She would have been on the receiving end of everything I felt! I guarantee it wouldn't have been anything nice between us! I went straight to the phone and called him. When he answered, he got more than an earful! He tried some lame excuse, like maybe it was the maintenance people, but we both knew that was B.S! I can only imagine what happened between them after my call, but he did know that she wouldn't have been able to withstand my wrath.

    Later that evening my friend D called, to tell me Bae called her to vent about the incident. He was upset at what "she" had done also. D tried to lighten the mood by repeating that he confided *he* didn't want to face me now either, but I wasn't laughing. I was battling voices in my head, telling me how to handle things. This only added fuel to the already deep-seated fire within me! The seed of bitterness, with all its cousins, had taken root in my heart, and was growing at an exponential rate. My heart and thoughts were darkening. After that incident, Bae stayed clear of me himself, and made sure she did too.

Note: Do you see how the hand of God moved? Only God can orchestrate such impeccable timing. Another ten seconds on that computer, and Sister Girl and I would have been face to face! Ten less seconds in the bathroom, and I would have caught her inside the house. If I had decided to search those parked cars outside, I probably would have found her hiding in one. Only God knows what would have happened then, but His saving Grace protected us both.

It was almost Thanksgiving, and Bae left a note telling me that he was going to visit his family for the Holiday. That confirmed two facts for me, first, that I would be alone, and second, that he felt no obligation towards me whatsoever. Of course I was angry, but I was angry all the time now. *Why tell me?*

Not long after he left, I heard in my mind to take my anointed oil and anoint the sofa and his bed. Ha! I ignored that completely! But in my quiet moments, I heard it again, then again. When I paid attention, I realized God was speaking to my spirit. I argued with God, questioning why I should. *Anything requiring anointing oil is for a blessing. I didn't want to bless him!* My arguing and questioning continued, but He never answered. Just the same instruction, anoint the sofa and his bed.

It took my angry rebellious self a couple days to relent, but I finally did what I was told. With attitude, I anointed it all—the bed, from post to post, the sheets, pillows, comforter, whatever was on the nightstand, and the rug around the bed. I anointed the sofa and the love seat, the throw pillows, the floor, the coffee table, the remote, anything he might touch. Then with self-righteous indignation, I announced to God that I had finished—I had done what He told me to do!

No response.

Bae was still my only connection in Florida, and the few days he was gone seemed like a really long time. It had only been three months since I arrived in Florida, where my whole life was turned upside-down, but *seemed like years!* I would often look at the Stranger in the mirror and wonder who she is. My solace was in overtime at work and loving on Smokey at home.

He had returned and was at the house when he called me. Surprised, I answered and was informed that he had just taken a stress test at the Dr.'s office, and was told to go straight to the hospital for further testing. He didn't seem alarmed in the least, and said that he was at home getting clothes. It sounded a bit unsettling to me though, so I told him I would take off from work to go with him. We weren't on good terms so he tried to resist. I'm sure he preferred his "girlfriend" to be there instead, but I pulled rank. The tests did not go well. Not only was he admitted on the spot, but scheduled for immediate surgery. We were told he had a blockage in his heart that required a stent (or two) to help the blood flow properly. We were both surprised to hear that! He filled out the paperwork and surgery prep began.

With that unexpected news, there was an awkward silence between us. My heart was filled with compassion and love, but in my head, I was angry and unforgiving. My mind told me it was his just punishment, and that he wasn't deserving of my love or compassion. But deep down, I did love him and wanted him to know, especially with him going into surgery. His countenance was stand-offish and unbothered, like I was a nuisance. So my pride shut my mouth, and my attitude took over. Normally, I would have prayed for him but I didn't do that either. I simply said, "See you later," understanding full well that *anything* could have happened. And with that, he was whisked away.

    I called my Mom to tell her about everything while I was waiting. Her sympathy for him had run its course. She didn't wish him ill, but she didn't want to hear his name again. In a very angry tone that I seldom heard from her, she made that quite clear. She told me she was tired of me talking about and defending some man who treated me like dirt and could care less about how I was getting along! She continued ranting for a moment, spewing all the things she had probably been holding in since that first night. When she was done, she drew the line, and threatened to hang up on me if I let his name ever come out of my mouth again while talking to her. *She was my best friend and confidant. How was I supposed to get through all of this if I couldn't talk to her?* Through her, I always found comfort, encouragement, and peace, but not now. What she said angered me, so I got off the phone. I figured I'd just wait it out alone. As I waited, her words rang in my ears, making me wonder what the root was to how Bae and I ended up here.

    I don't remember how long the surgery lasted, but when the surgeon came out looking for "Mrs. Bae" I stood up. I don't think I will ever forget his words to me. In short, he told me Bae was a "lucky man" and that *Somebody* was on his side. The blockage was severe, and if he had had a heart attack, he would have been dead before he even hit the ground. Then he repeated that he was a lucky man. As soon as I heard those words the second time, I immediately heard God say, "*That's* why I told you to anoint the sofa and his bed." The Lord's words reverberated through my chest like when you're standing close to a fireworks finale. I was so ashamed! I ran outside and wept. I could do nothing but apologize, repent, and beg God for forgiveness. I was overwhelmed with remorse and gratitude. My mind played out different scenarios that could have taken place. My stubbornness or disobedience could have cost his life, but his blood would have been on my hands! *Could I have lived with that*? Of course I was outraged about everything, but if the worst had happened, would my anger even matter? Wouldn't I then be lost in grief? I thought of the scripture, "Behold, to obey is better than sacrifice, and to hearken than the fat of rams" (1 Samuel 15:22). *I'm so sorry Lord.*

    Thank God, Bae came through surgery safely. I don't think he ever knew God used me to spare his life back then. I never told him about it. But, I knew instantly when God spoke at the hospital that things could have turned out another way. There was a great shaking and humbling within me. In all my messiness, God was not only with me, but using me. All I could do was thank Him for His Goodness towards me…and Bae.

    Note: Many times, we are hindered by our emotions. Having eyes, we do not see, and having ears, we do not hear. We prevent our own maturation in faith (Christ) because of pettiness, and miss out on understanding the deeper things of God. I know I did.

After all these years, is it possible that my move to Florida was never at all for what I thought it was? Is it possible that God allowed my move because I had that assignment yet to fulfill? (Remember what drew me to Bae in the beginning.) I may not be able to definitively answer those questions, but I know what I heard God say at that hospital. I'm convinced that had I not anointed the house like God told me to, I may be sharing a different kind of testimony—one filled with guilt and regret.

Despite that whole incident, nothing changed between us. It was as if nothing ever happened. He stayed with her and I resented him all the more—especially knowing what I knew. Then, another calamitous blow. The housing market crashed, and the sale of my house fell through! I hadn't paid December's mortgage, per my realtor's advice because we were scheduled to close that month. Turned out, the other realtor and buyer were attempting something "unorthodox", ultimately resulting in the dissolution of the sale. My realtor didn't find any of this out until after the holidays, which meant I now had two mortgage payments due, December and January. But I was still in deep debt from my relocation! My saving grace was supposed to be the sale of my house and the plan Bae and I had set up. All of that was null and void now, and the debt was mine alone to pay.

(I didn't find out till much later that the money the buyer forfeited when the contract fell through, was *taken* by my realtor. Easy to do when the client is "trapped" in another state).

Atop two mortgage payments, the monthly house bills were due too. To say I was stressed, is a gross under statement. I was way beyond that! I was drowning, suffocating. I was barely surviving. There was so much month at the end of the money, it seemed as if I was never paid at all! I lost all my weight. My hair was falling out by the handful, and I was very much depressed and apathetic.

Then *God* prompted me to email Bae and tell him that I forgive him. *Nope! Absolutely not! God, why should I reach out to him when he should be reaching out to me asking for my forgiveness?* That didn't make any sense to me! I complained that God always *made* me go back and fix *my* mistakes, so Him telling me to make the first step when I was the one wronged, was unfair to me! I wasn't having it! In my eyes, it was a double standard and I didn't like it one bit! *Why should I forgive him after everything he's done to me? And why are **You** telling me, knowing what he did?*

(All my years of salvation and not one of the scriptures I knew came into mind: Luke 6:37, "forgive, and you shall be forgiven"; Matthew 6:14-15, "For if ye forgive men their trespasses, your heavenly Father will also forgive you: But if ye forgive not men their trespasses, neither will your Father forgive your trespasses"; Matthew 5:44, "Love your enemies, bless them that curse you, do good to them that hate you, pray for them which despitefully use you and persecute you.")

I was so outraged, my thinking was distorted. I was hurt, stubborn, and prideful. I had several tantrums over this, but every time I'd calm down, I'd hear the same thing again ...."Tell him you forgive him."

"*NO!*" I was so far gone. I was too heated; too busy murmuring and complaining—just angry! I couldn't recognize God trying to help me in this situation. But oh, the sweet loving Grace and Mercy of God! He kept trying to reach me to wake me up. He knew how to turn everything around. He knew how to make a way when I saw none; how to open a closed door, and how to shut the door on the enemy. He knew how to favor me and send someone to bless me in my need. God wasn't caught off guard by any of this. Only I was! My eyes were blind and my ears were deaf. And now...my heart was shattered! *How could I be rational?*

> *If ever there was a time I wanted to stop following and believing God, it was now!*"

It felt like He was more concerned about Bae than for me. Every time He spoke to me, it had to do with Bae! I was ticked about that too! Surely God watched this whole thing play out! *I* was the one wronged here! *I* was the one losing everything! And suffering! If ever there was a time I wanted to stop following and believing God, it was now! *HE was turning on me!*

It took another week for me to even accept what the Lord said. Still huffing, I eventually wrote and rewrote the email many times before I considered it to be "nicety," (nice but nasty). In short, I apologized, asked for forgiveness, and gave him mine. It was done, but now I needed to actually send it. Especially feeling he didn't deserve it, this particular task was extremely difficult. I was very emotional about it. I felt I would appear weak and vulnerable. *He certainly didn't seem bothered by what he had done to me, so why would he care about my forgiveness?* I battled with this so much in my head, I gave myself a serious headache. I sat in front of the computer for a long time in mental conflict. *Just do it,* I thought. So, letting God know that I felt *forced* into obedience, I hit the SEND button, immediately regretting it. But I couldn't take it back, so I had to pretend to be OK with it to remain sane—but I was not happy.

A few days went by before I saw an email from him. I was nervous about it because I had no idea what to expect. I felt I understood how that line between love and hate is so thin. The battle within me was real! My thought was, *If I don't like what I read, do I let him know he messed with the wrong one, or do I let it go because I love him?* I really wanted him to experience *something* that would be the equivalent to the devastation I was experiencing. There was love and revenge in my heart, both of equal proportion. My inner me meant business! I was wrestling with that question when I opened the email. I closed my eyes and took a deep breath before starting to read. I can't tell you what it said, I don't remember it all now. It was a short response, not what I was hoping for. What it did say was that he "*forgave me* a long time ago." WHAT!? Never once did he apologize for anything he did, didn't do, said or didn't say—like this was all just some *trivial* misunderstanding! I read it a few times because I was having trouble believing what my eyes were seeing, or in this case, *weren't* seeing. Then I was enraged all over again! I verbally took back any forgiveness I had extended him, deeming him unworthy. Then I started fussing at God! I ranted to Him about what I thought was Bae's arrogant tone in the email—where I felt he implied that I was the one that needed forgiveness! And his oh so short and nonchalant response—*like he didn't do anything wrong!* I was furious because I felt God *made* me open a door, only to have it slammed in my face! I was p*ssed! *He didn't need my forgiveness? He didn't need to apologize to me for anything?* I kept reminding God that I told Him I didn't want to do it! I didn't want to write to him! I didn't want to reach out to him! *He* should have been the one reaching out to me! It should have been *him* making the first step! *Him* apologizing! *Him* asking for forgiveness! *Him* trying to make amends! I had worked myself into great fury.

I thought, *God is my enemy's friend.*

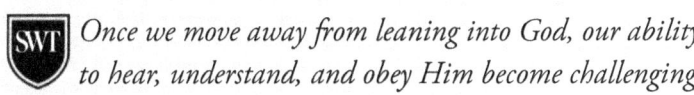 *Once we move away from leaning into God, our ability to hear, understand, and obey Him become challenging.*

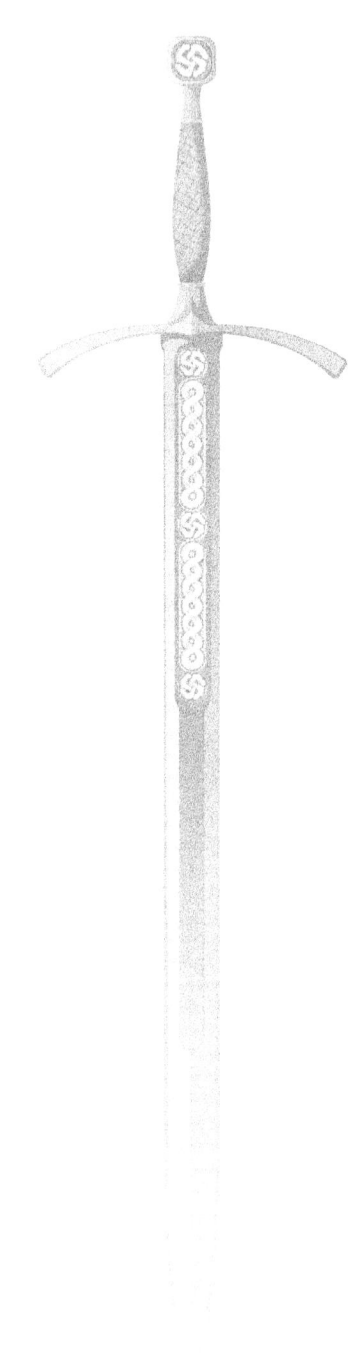

CHAPTER

PIVOT
An About Face

I was at my wit's end! I was tired of enduring all I was going through. Before, I was happy, healthy, and doing well. I had a good career, some money, friends, my family, and a beautiful home. Less than one year later, all of that changed! My money was gone and I was in overwhelming debt, scraping to survive in a place where I had no friends, no family, and no help. I was in arrears with my house and no longer had prospective buyers due to the rapidly declining market. I was one hour away from my job going north, and an hour away from church going south. I looked haggard and disheveled. I was losing my house—*my house*. The one I fought my Ex for!

The house God gave me! The solo accomplishment of my career. *MY HOUSE!* A myriad of emotions regularly swirled around my head. I felt duped, humiliated, rejected, isolated and abandoned. I could barely think of anything else. I stewed over every detail from my first meeting Bae to our last day. I thought of how much I had done for him. How I helped him. Supported him. CARRIED HIM! I wondered *why* he was so thoughtless, careless and selfish. What lie he concocted to explain me to that Chick. His utter cowardice! How could he just dis me and treat me like garbage? This whole thing could have been prevented. He had every opportunity to speak up before I left Cali…but he didn't. *Punk!*

The losses in my life kept accumulating. I lost my house (that broke me). *Did Bae ever love me? Had he only used me? Was his goal to destroy me?* My thoughts began changing. No matter what I was doing, these thoughts circulated in my head nonstop. Once I added everything up. Including my move, the loss of my house, and the portion of my retirement I had to withdraw to survive, I lost over $600,000.00. That's right, SIX HUNDRED THOUSAND DOLLARS! The number kept ringing in my ears. *Six. The number of man in the Bible. Man. That's what he was… "a man". A man that tried to ruin me! A man that purposely disrupted my life, then left me!* Life before him kept crossing my mind. It wasn't perfect but it was *mine*. I was good. Now everyday, I was grappling for a breath of air. I simply couldn't wrap my mind

> *Life before him kept crossing my mind. It wasn't perfect but it was mine.*

around it. But I was tired of that *coward* impersonating a man! I was sick of his running and dodging and doing whatever he pleased at *my* expense! Living like he was king, forgetting all I had done for him!

    A good man, a decent man, would have done things differently. He would have sat me down and explained things. Even though it would have *hurt* me, I would have respected him for his honesty and integrity. In spite of his other relationship, he should have helped me until I got back on my feet. I am here because of him! He owed me that! He uprooted me with false dreams and promises that were all lies! He had plenty of opportunities to stop me from coming; to handle things differently. A man is supposed to provide, protect, and cover his woman. He's a fixer. He should have protected me and covered me, even though we weren't together, until I could stand again on my own! He should have talked to me and given me some closure for my peace of mind. At least leave me like you found me! Where is his accountability? Surely he doesn't think paying the bills was his only responsibility! No, he took the easy way out—coward! He left me to pick up all the pieces! I was flabbergasted. I meant nothing at all, to a man that meant so much to me….

    Ha! Ok, but Tuesday's coming! He's gonna stop by like usual, barely speak, pick up his mail, get clothes, and whatever else, (I'm sure, all things I bought him!), to take to her house. Then sashay out the door to his happy new life like he owes me nothing! Humph, I don't think so! **This** *Tuesday will be different!* **This** *Tuesday, he doesn't get to disrespect me anymore! No more running! No more hiding! No more ignoring me! Disregarding me! Nah,* **this** *Tuesday, we're gonna talk like two* *grown adults.* You're *gonna sit down and tell me everything I've been wanting to know since last year. Then, you may leave!*

I had made up my mind; it was decided. *Tuesday is going to be D-day!*

 Dearly beloved, avenge not yourselves, but rather give place unto wrath: for it is written, Vengeance is mine; I will repay, saith the Lord.

CHAPTER 5

THE RECKONING
Eye for an Eye

It's Tuesday! And I called in sick. Bae liked to come over when I wasn't home so I wasn't going to take the chance of missing him. Today, he would be surprised to see me at home; the same way *she* was when she showed up uninvited! Normally, I'd get home in the afternoons around 5ish pm. He would have already come and gone, but occasionally, he'd stop by sometime after 7pm too. He'd stroll in all arrogant and proud. He'd acknowledge me, maybe make small talk, but I didn't like the pacification. *Don't come up in here shootin' the breeze like all is well between us. If you wanna talk, talk to me about the real problem, otherwise shut the * up!*

My love-hate relationship for him was intense. The sight of his face sickened me, but I still longed to see it. I disliked how his presence disrupted my peace, but I still wanted him around. I wouldn't believe anything he said, but I still wanted him to talk to me. I couldn't understand myself—how could l hate him so, and love him so much at the same time? Yet it was my sad truth… *Whatever time he comes today won't make any difference—I have all day. This day, I have the patience of Job.*

Smokey napped peacefully on the balcony. All was calm and quiet outside. It was a beautiful day. Inside though, it was different. Almost every light in the house was on. Some random channel played louder than usual on the television, and since he hadn't stopped by before his shift, I had the radio blasting so I could formulate a tentative timeline of his arrival after sign off.

I was wearing a pair of blue jeans and a t-shirt, with my tennis shoes laced up nice and tight. My hair was pulled back and tied up into a small bun. I was in "fight mode" just in case. I rummaged around in my closet and his closet till I finally found what I was looking for. Alas! Feeling satisfied and prepared, I sat in that familiar big white chair facing the door, listening to the radio, with a loaded shotgun across my lap and a .22 caliber under my right thigh.

I envisioned him submitting to my demands while in total shock that he had pushed *me* so far to the brink. I imagined all the lame answers he would give while simultaneously trying to placate me. I chuckled to myself imagining all the B.S. about to unfold, but this time knowing I had the upper hand. So I eagerly but patiently waited for my time to come. I felt a rush of adrenaline when I heard him sign off. I began counting down the minutes to his *surprise welcome*, while remembering the surprise welcome I received when I arrived last August. Part of me was giddy with anticipation and anxiety; the other part of me was disturbed and suppressing deep pain.

He's late! His scheduled window of arrival had come and gone. Not wanting to give up, I imagined he was held up at the station with unexpected work, so I waited for the eight o'clock hour instead. I was disappointed but determined, so I waited…and waited…and waited. Shortly before 9:30 pm, I figured he wasn't coming. Furious, I turned off the radio, and the unnecessary lights. I put the shotgun back where it belonged, but kept the .22 with me in case he showed up anyway. Then I sat on the couch facing the TV, with a drink in my hand, mumbling obscenities, trying to settle my nerves and come down from the adrenaline high. Around 11pm., I resolved that *he escaped again.*

I knew I wouldn't sleep much, but I still had to go to work in the morning. It was time for bed.

The devil had me! Payback dominated my thinking. *He messed over the wrong one!* I wanted to ruin Bae the same way he ruined me! There were things I could have done naturally. I could have destroyed all the things I had bought him. I could have caused problems at his job, maybe even gotten him fired. I considered selling his collection of celebrities' memorabilia to recoup some of my monetary losses. But despite my efforts to ignore Him, I would hear the Lord speaking, saying, "Vengeance is mine; I will repay.(Romans 12:19). HE said, *"You* are to 'Love your enemies, pray for those who use you…' (Matthew 5:44)

I'm not trying to hear that God. You take too long!

I don't want You to repay—I wanna do it!

It took days for me to calm down; I was so angry. With every vicious thought I had, God would simply say, "No." HE was always *interfering* in my thought process! I finally snapped, "Fine! I won't do anything, but You have to bring him back." That was my deal.

Note: There is so much to talk about here, but let me begin by telling you Bae never came back to the house again while I was living there. (If he did, I never knew it). God had stepped in yet again, saving *me*, and him! I'm sure you can imagine all the possible scenarios that could have unfolded in an encounter like the one I had planned. I was definitely not in my right mind. Allowing those negative thoughts, opened a door to the enemy's evil schemes. My anger, bitterness, and resentment had such a hold on me, that I was "happier" with God not speaking. (To be honest with you, I wasn't checking for God because I held Him somewhat responsible for all of this, but we'll talk about that a bit later).

In all my craziness though, God *never* left me. At the time, I didn't see how God had protected me that *Tuesday*. Today I know and can tell you without a doubt, I believe things would have gone another way that night. In spite of feeling in control, I believe I would have been totally hijacked by the devil! The potential magnitude of error was plentiful. But God saved my behind! Had Bae come that night, one or both of us, could be dead or imprisoned to this day! What the devil meant for evil, God turned it around for good.

Nobody but God can discern the thoughts and intents of the heart. 1 Samuel states: "*… for the Lord does* *not see as man sees; for man looks at the outward appearance, but the Lord looks at the heart."* Only God knew what was inside me. "A jury of my peers" would have effortlessly convicted me of premeditated murder. I wouldn't have been able to convince anyone otherwise. God alone, knew my pain, my intention, and my heart towards Bae. I can tell you I loved that man, with everything I had, and everything I was. I *never* intended to harm him in any way, but I knew no one would have ever believed that, especially because I was waiting, and armed with a shotgun and a twenty-two. It probably would have been labeled "a crime of passion." My life, and his life, could be dramatically different, or over, if not for the Grace and Love of Almighty God. Because of Him, our lives continue, and I'm able to share this story with you.

  *In all my craziness though, God **never** left me.*

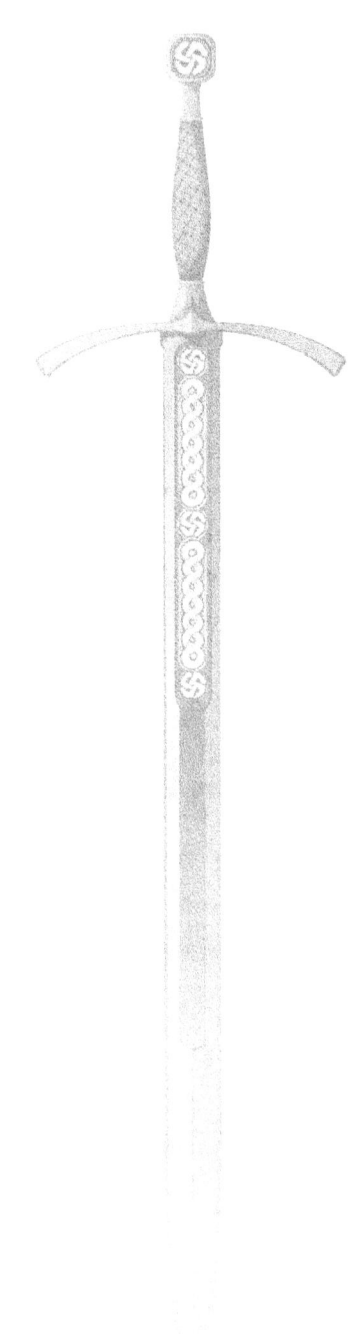

THE PROCESS
Heartache to Healing

My heart desperately wants you to comprehend the depth in which God loves and cares for you. Remembering that story, truly enlightened my understanding of God's Love. Know that whatever has happened in your life; regardless of what you've done; no matter how far you've strayed; even if you've never known Him for yourself before, God is *always* ready to receive you—His arms open wide. Cling to Him! HE IS LOVE. He will *never* leave you nor forsake you (Hebrews 13:5). It is He that created you. You are not here by accident. Simply open your heart and just whisper the Name, Jesus. He will answer.

Too often, God is blamed for things He's not responsible for. I was no different. I was mad at Him and blamed Him for everything that happened to me. I mentioned earlier that during that pivotal time, I held Him partially responsible for my collapse. I wasn't checking for Him. My attitude and behavior towards God at that time was shocking. I'm not proud of it, but I hope my transparency will better help you understand what I said in the above paragraph, about His love, kindness, and compassion. I'm praying you will receive revelation in different areas of your own life as you continue reading about mine.

I told you Bae never came back to the house again. He never came back to me either. Months passed, and one day he emailed me telling me I had to move out when the lease was up. You can imagine my choice of words for him! I couldn't afford to go anywhere. My life was still in shambles and I was a total wreck. It enraged me that Bae was happily continuing his life while I struggled. Unbeknownst to me though, God was with me, and had me covered. By the time the lease was up, I was able to get my own place on the other side of the complex with no down payment, no deposit, and no credit check, (even with the recent foreclosure of my house)! God still favored me. My neighbor pitied me and moved all my belongings, (a four bedroom house), from the storage facility to my new place…*and* set everything up for me! *One* man lifted and loaded over sixty boxes and all my heavy furniture onto a U-haul, then unloaded it, and carried it all up three flights of stairs! God protected him from injury, and graced him with stamina and strength to complete the job *alone*, in just one day! The topper was, I didn't have to pay him one dime and he never asked for a thing. (Thank you Smiley. I will never forget your kindness). God had blessed me tremendously, but I still couldn't see it because my bitterness was like blinders over my eyes.

After the move, I found several boxes missing, but the deadline to file a claim had long since passed. I should have felt better in my own place; lighter, less burdened. Instead, I felt insurmountable pressure from every side. It seemed every move brought a different set of problems. Reality setting in, I was on my own. I couldn't focus on anything. There was no attachment to Bae now. He was gone. And I was grieving.

Note: I don't believe that the grieving process is only for the deceased. I understand it is usually associated with death, but a broken heart is a broken heart. I know how I grieved over this relationship, and how it took years to get through it. My heart was broken for a long time.

Today, it's known as Takotsubo Cardiomyopathy or Broken-heart Syndrome. When a person experiences an extremely traumatic emotional or physical event, a surge of stress hormones is released into the body with the potential to cause short-term heart failure, which of course, can be fatal.

People handle losses differently, so one event can totally change a person's life. This could range in any area from any accident, to a divorce, to the loss of a loved one. So neither male nor female, young nor old, fit nor healthy, is exempt.

When a person's heart is broken, they experience a continuous aching. It is an excruciatingly deep inward pain that has profound traumatic effects on the person's psyche and their physical body. It's a level of pain that cannot be seen with the natural eye. What is seen by others and often misunderstood, are the physical symptoms or effects manifesting on the outside.

The road to recovery is not an easy one, and unfortunately, some don't ever recover. It's not like a band aid will help, or a scab will develop in a few days. There is no medicine or antibiotic you can take to alleviate the pain or help you heal quicker. You must go through a process to get to the other side of grief. Whatever issues are tormenting the mind will supersede everything else. Therefore it's my opinion that the mind has to be liberated before the heart can be. Because we're still dealing with loss, I believe a person has to fight through the various grieving stages of denial, anger, bargaining, depression, and acceptance before experiencing any real healing. Hence, I submit to you that the stages of the grieving process are the same, whether grieving for the dead or for the living.

> *A person has to fight through the various grieving stages of denial, anger, bargaining, depression, and acceptance before experiencing any real healing.*

Every day it felt like my wheels were turning, but I wasn't moving. I busied myself with work and unpacking, although I was still very isolated and broken. My coworkers tried to rally around me at work, but couldn't change anything for me inwardly. God sent a couple "friends" as company, but ultimately I was trapped inside in deep anguish and agony. My family was miles away. None of them wanted to hear my constant crying every time they called, so although they checked on me, calls were less frequent. My sister came out once to help me unpack and keep me company. I cried a lot. She did her best to console me, but it was a tall order. Although it was short lived, it was nice having her there. Once she left, my outlet was gone, except for the grocery store or maybe the gas station.

I had no church home either—I had stopped going. No matter, I wasn't speaking to God anymore anyway. Except for the cat, I was alone 98% of the time, going through my own personal hell. I thought, *Is this what life is? Headache and heartache all the time? A constant battle to survive? Never getting ahead? Why do I want to be here? What is the point?*

It wasn't the first time suicidal thoughts had entered my mind. Usually I fought them off with ease, but I had no peace now. The never ending cerebral battle began to take its toll on me. I was crumbling in spirit, soul, and body. I couldn't see my way out and I didn't have "a reason" for anything. Those demonic thoughts swirled in my mind more often than not, and I slowly began to entertain different ideas more and more.

One evening I was sitting on the couch, watching television. I was minding my own business when out of the blue I heard, "I love you." It was loud, like someone was in the room with me but I knew I was home alone. I was startled for a moment, then recognized the Voice and responded aloud, "You don't love me! If You did, You would have never let him do that to me!" I kept it short and to the point. As far as I was concerned, the discussion was over—I wasn't tryna talk to *Him* anyway!

My peace was now disturbed and I was flustered. I desperately wanted to ignore those words, but they lingered in my mind. I was determined to be stubborn, so I fought it off. I don't know how much time went by, but I had just started to relax when I heard Him again, "I love you."

This time I performed! I was like a child having a temper tantrum! I put my hands over my ears and yelled, "La la la la la! I don't wanna hear *You*! You *don't* love me! You *let* him do everything to me and *You* could have stopped it! *You* should have protected me! You could have *made* him do the right thing! *You don't love me*, and I don't wanna hear it! Ahhhhhh, la la la la!"

With that, I slammed the doors to my heart and mind, determined to ignore the Lord. Per my request, I didn't hear from Him again.

Note: Despite my disrespectful attitude, God stayed with me. He knew I was in deep distress mentally, and broken in heart and spirit. He knew about this trial I would face before it ever took place! I knew He knew—it's why I lashed out at Him.

When we don't listen, God allows things to happen in our lives that we do not foresee or understand. He may try to correct us along the way, but we usually have our own agenda in mind. We want what we want. If God isn't saying what we want to hear, we act like we don't hear Him. We convince ourselves that He will bless what we've decided to do because we know He loves us.

Well, I had my own agenda too. There were signs, indications things weren't right before I left Cali, but *I* had already arranged my future, without checking with God. *I* had set everything in motion, never thinking twice if I was doing what pleased Him. I felt the "blessing part" should have been easy for Him, because *I* had done all the work. Not even understanding I was out of His will, led me down a long, dark, and dangerous path. But God knew what the enemy was doing. I shake my head when I think of how things could have turned out...but for the Grace of God! He's so very kind and compassionate, forgiving and merciful. I could have died in my sins and been lost forever, but He protected me and loved me until I found my way back. **There is no greater Love!**

My life was still a monstrous bundle of chaos and confusion. I couldn't make sense of anything. Everything was tangled and mixed up together, like when the chain of a necklace gets terribly twisted and knotted into a ball. I'll admit three years later, I was still very agitated and frustrated because I had no explanation; no understanding of what initially caused the relationship to fall apart. There was no closure for me. Bae and I never spoke again. I questioned myself repeatedly—my intellect, my judgment, my worth. I lost my confidence and decisiveness. I was so far removed from who I used to be, I didn't recognize myself. I was mad at the world so I never saw God subtly working in me. His sweet Holy Spirit kept tugging at my hardened heart. I had enough head knowledge to know that only God could fill the void in my life. But I still had an attitude towards Him. I knew God could fix things. I knew He could fix me, but I was stubborn and didn't want to talk to Him. *He was still to blame.*

My drive to and from work was approximately one hour each way. That was a lot of time for my idle mind to wander. I kept a headache from thinking too much. Nothing could quiet my mind for that distance of time, but I knew prayer could. Problem was, in my arrogance, I had nothing to say to God. *He had failed me. And that's not supposed to be what "love does." He should know that since HE wrote the Book!*

The enemy was still lurking around, planting seeds of my demise. I knew what could combat that, but I was battling two *bigger* issues. First, I didn't *want* to talk to God. I was still angry with Him, and praying meant I had to. Second, I didn't want to get so caught up in prayer that I heard myself praising Him or asking Him for any help. So… what did *I* do? My sassy genius self decided I would fill those driving hours by praying in the *spirit!*

The Bible clearly states in 1 Corinthians 14:2 (NKJV), that he that speaks in *an unknown tongue*, speaks not to men, but to God: for no man understands him; but in the spirit he speaks *mysteries*.

An "unknown tongue" is a prayer language that allows the believer to speak *directly to* God. After Salvation, it is available to every born again believer (it is different from the tongues spoken of in 1 Corinthians 12).

A "mystery" in the Bible, is a hidden secret or a truth that cannot be understood by man, without *revelation from God*.

So in my infinite wisdom, I did the very thing I was so determined not to do! I spoke directly to God through the Holy Spirit, who interceded for me. 1 Corinthians 3:19b (CEB) states, "As it is written, He catches the wise in their cleverness." (Lol, I hope you see the humor in that!)

Somewhere during this routine of driving and praying in the spirit five to six days a week, my attitude began to change. I didn't realize it at first, so I can't tell you exactly when it happened. I didn't notice the tumultuous ball of my life began unraveling and slowly lining up. I wasn't consumed with my situation or my pain every second of the day. In fact, I began to interact with people more. Occasionally, I found myself giggling, even laughing from time to time. Eventually, it dawned on me that I could get through a day without tears. I was taken aback by this myself because I had been stuck in that pit for so long, the change startled even me! But then I smiled, inviting the return of the person I had lost years ago. I noticed myself getting stronger mentally and physically. My eyes opened and I began to see how to maneuver around some of the obstacles in my life. I wasn't in denial anymore, but I still had vengeful thoughts. I was still angry, but not as bitter. I can't say that I was happy, but I was no longer depressed. Those suicidal (and homicidal) thoughts finally disappeared. Deep down, I knew it was because of my constant praying in the spirit to the Lord, but I didn't openly want to admit that. Romans 8:26-27 (NLT) states, "And the Holy Spirit helps us in our weakness. For example, we don't know what God wants us to pray for. But the Holy Spirit prays for us with groanings that cannot be expressed with words. (v.27) And the Father who knows all hearts knows what the Spirit is saying, for the Spirit pleads for us believers in harmony with God's own will."

  I was tired of feeling worthless and dead inside. I had sunken to a point where I couldn't free myself, and nobody else could help. It was only the complete and unconditional Love of God that kept me from what the enemy had plotted against me. Although I turned my back on Him,

He never once left my side. I was grateful that He pulled me up out of the muck and mire. Thank You Jesus, for saving my soul; for saving my life! You are truly the friend that sticks closer than a brother (Proverbs 18:24).

The recovery process in my natural circumstances remained because my grieving had displaced it. I had not been concerned with the physical world around me, because I was in a mental crisis, and I simply didn't care. It was normal for me to have past due bills and little to no gas in the car. I had no real desire for food, company, or entertainment. I had no family, few friends, and worked just enough not to lose my job. I had retreated from life. But by praying, I finally understood that God's Grace had sustained me during those years.

New Life was being breathed into me again! I knew it on the inside. I was stronger in my mind, body, and spirit. I felt the shift in my thinking and had more strength in my physical body. The mindset of shame, low self-esteem, and self worth began to leave. I wasn't tired all the time and experienced real periods of peace. Glimmers of joy started disrupting the darkness of my mind, the way a bolt of lightning temporarily illuminates the sky. I began remembering who I am. I am a child of The King! (Psalm 149:2) I am fearfully and wonderfully made! (Psalm 139:14) I am the apple of His eye! (Proverbs 7:2) I was grateful! Grateful to the Holy Spirit, who watched over me and interceded on my behalf! Grateful for the astronomical price Jesus paid on the Cross! Grateful that, despite my many flaws and shortcomings, God loves me anyway, and He never stopped!

I was humbled, full, and missed my relationship with my Heavenly Father. How it must have grieved Him to see me in such a fallen state.

    I prayed now because I wanted to! I sought Him because I missed Him and needed Him! The more I prayed, the stronger I became. There was a shifting that took place - in my mindset, my actions, and my atmosphere. And for the first time in a long while, hope arose on the inside. Though the weapon had formed against me, it did not prosper (Isaiah 54:17). Hallelujah! I wanted my strength back; my health back; my joy back—I wanted my *life* back!

 The mind has to be liberated before the heart can be.

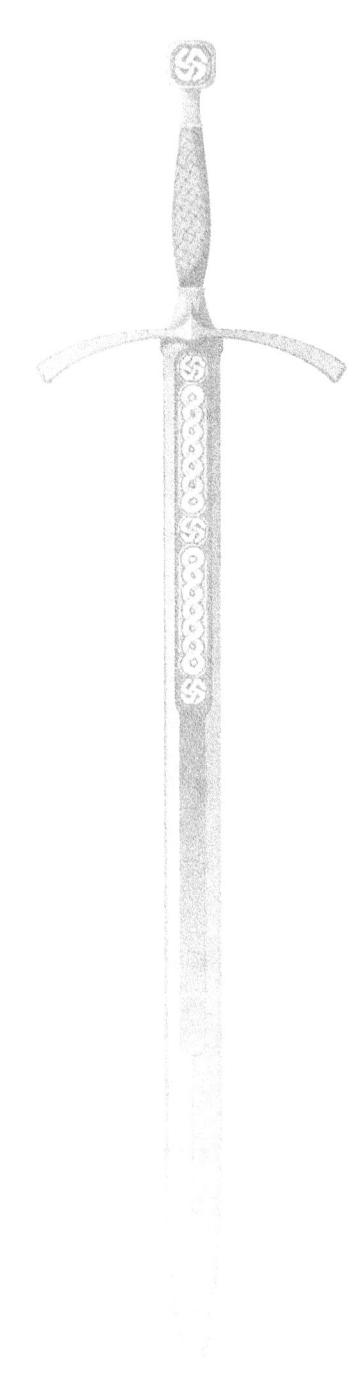

THE BLIND SEE
Insight and Understanding

I previously stated that I was still bothered because I had no closure. I had been good to Bae and loved him with every part of me. Because of that, a huge void remained in my understanding. I tried not to dwell on it because it had great potential to hinder my healing progress, but spoken or unspoken, it was yet "unsettled" in my heart and mind. I also mentioned some paragraphs back, that praying in the spirit reveals mysteries, or a hidden secret or truth that can't be understood by man, without revelation from God. Keeping those two things in mind, I want to share with you what happened next.

The day was like most other days. It was hot, and my windows were down as I drove home from work. Listening to gospel music and praying in the spirit, I was enjoying my ride home and spending time with the Lord. It had become routine now and oftentimes the drive didn't seem to be long enough. As I was praying, I was interrupted by a gentle but stern Voice, that said, "You put him before Me." For a split second I was startled. It sounded like someone was sitting next to me in the car. I hadn't heard God audibly since the time I argued with Him about loving me.

Instinctively, I responded immediately. I said, "No I di…", then I caught myself immediately and thought, *GOD is speaking!* So I said aloud, "Of course I did. Lord, I'm sorry." I apologized outwardly, but internally I wasn't convinced that it was true. I needed to think about it—as if I could somehow disprove what GOD said. I definitely didn't think I had put Bae before Him. I was serving Him the whole time. I never missed going to church. I even sang in three different choirs there! I tithed, read my Bible, prayed, and fellowshipped. What else could I do? *I was serving Him!* But the Holy Spirit invaded my thoughts and rebuked me! God's way is perfect! HE is not a man that He should lie, Nor a son of man, that HE should repent (Psalm 18:30; Numbers 23:19 AMP).

For the rest of the ride, I was mulling over what I heard, secretly looking for "loop holes" to defend myself. Not long after I walked in the front door, my actions over the past years played in my mind like a movie.

Once Bae and I started dating, I still attended church and sang regularly, but I was not focused on God. Yes, I prayed, read the Bible, and tithed too, but it became routine, rather than reverencing. As time passed, much of that shifted as well. It wasn't just my routine changing, *I* was changing! God told me He was not first; HE had been displaced—that I had given "my heart to another." (This is now full circle from Chapter One and my Ex.) Instantly, I understood why God was not pleased. And with that, the Holy Spirit rested His case.

Eyes wide open, I could comprehend the many reasons my downward spiral began years ago. Once that revelation burst forth, I was completely ashamed. The first commandment states, "Thou shalt have no other gods before Me." (Exodus 20:3; Deuteronomy 5:7). The truth was, I had put a *man* before God, and centered my life around him. I no longer held God in the highest esteem, or honored Him the way I should have. I had not reverenced my Creator for who He is!

It may not have been what I wanted to hear, but it was certainly what I needed to know. A "mystery" had been revealed to me, and my understanding was illuminated. The blinders were removed, and everything was clear. I had no hiding place. I cried aloud to the Lord in repentance, asking for forgiveness for putting anybody or anything above Him. I wept bitterly because I understood how good He had been to me. How He had covered me, rescued me, and saved me from *total* destruction and devastation, even though I had turned my back on Him. I saw how the devil had set me up, and the grim reality of how differently things could have turned out. I was appalled at my poor judgment, arrogance, and stupidity. It was hard to look at myself in the mirror.

Note: Have you ever repeatedly beaten yourself up over a mistake you knew you should have known better about? That's what I was doing. The air had been knocked out of me and I had no fight left. I *wanted* to run and hide. But where can you hide from the presence of the Lord? The self condemnation was staggering! Notwithstanding, this truth needed to be revealed to me so I could repent from the heart and be cleansed. To be righteous again before Him, I needed a *"proper"* realignment. Embarrassed and ashamed, I struggled to pray, but I pressed in anyway. Each day became a bit easier. And this time, I prayed with a clean heart, in the strength of the Lord.

It's my own term, so let me tell you what "proper" realignment means.

Well, "agreement" itself, is a potent weapon in the Kingdom. In Matthew 18:19, the Bible speaks on the *power* of agreement between two believers. Ecclesiastes 4:12, speaks about the *strength* of a threefold cord.

With what I was coming out of, I needed power and strength. It wasn't enough for me to just have my heart and mouth agree because my mind would wander. It did no good to have my mind and mouth agree if my heart wavered. It certainly wouldn't matter if my heart and mind agreed, if my mouth inadvertently spoke the contrary. I had to get my mind, my heart, and my mouth to line up together. *That* was the threefold cord! I needed to make up my mind, settle things in my heart, then speak the Word (in faith), for my circumstances to change. It wasn't easy. It took commitment, tenacity, and fortitude. And so it also does today. These two trifectas, (heart, mind, and mouth; commitment, tenacity, and fortitude), break chains and move mountains!

The hardest hurdle to overcome was learning to forgive myself. With my personality, I struggled with that for a long while. My idiocy replayed on a loop in my head. It was the enemy's effort to keep me bound through guilt and shame, but the Holy Spirit would remind me of His goodness. He would bring scripture verses to my remembrance like: "There is therefore now no condemnation to them which are in Christ Jesus, who walk not after the flesh, but after the Spirit" (Romans 8:1); "The Lord is compassionate and gracious, slow to anger, abounding in love; He does not treat us as our sins deserve or repay us according to our iniquities; as far as the east is from the west, so far has He removed our transgressions from us" (Psalm 103:8,10,12 NIV); "Though your sins be as scarlet, they shall be white as snow…" (Isaiah 1:18); "I, even I, am He who blots out your transgressions for My own sake; And I will not remember your sins" (Isaiah 43:25 NKJV). Although I couldn't necessarily see it or feel it happening, it was spiritual food for my soul, encouraging me, strengthening me, and healing me day to day. God *never* once left me! So now that I was reachable, and teachable, He began to bring me out.

    Child of God, there may be a time in life when you feel unworthy of forgiveness. Perhaps you think God will not or cannot forgive you, so you don't ask. Instead of running to Him for help, you run away from Him in fear or shame. I've felt that way many times before so I understand. That is why I can tell you that's *not* who He is! *He's not like man.* His love for you is eternal. He is faithful to His Word and *always* ready to forgive a repentant heart. He's full of mercy to those who call upon Him (Psalm 86:5). Go to Him, all who are burdened and heavy laden, and He will give you rest (Matthew 11:28). It's His promise.

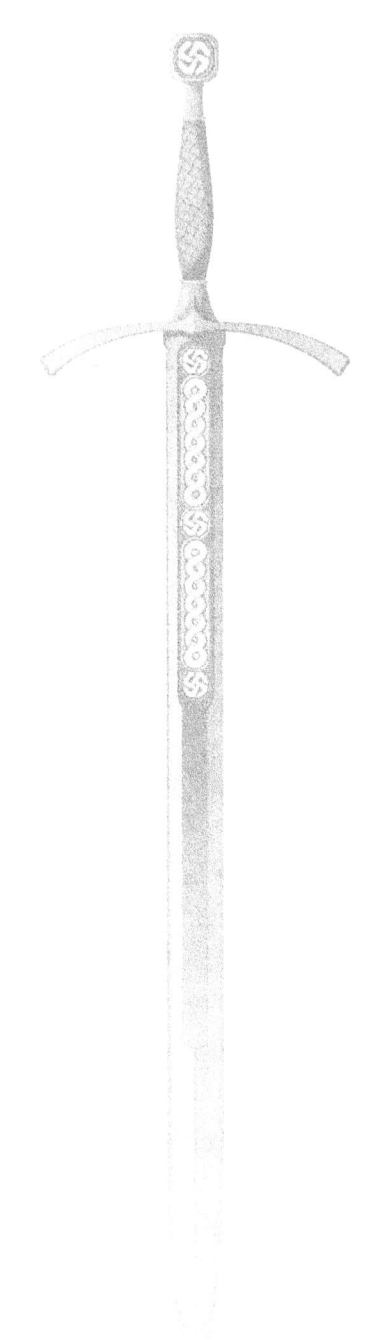

CHURCH HURT
Wounding the Injured

I want to transition here and say a little something about this very touchy subject for a moment because it plays a big role today with Christians and non-Christians alike. It played a role when I was going through my ordeal too, and I remember it well.

Most people have heard the term "church hurt" before, but what is it? Church Hurt is an emotional or physical pain to someone, through words, actions, or inactions, from a person representing the church. It is real pain or trauma, and can range along a broad spectrum of incidents like, hurtful words from a member, to gross actions from the Pastor. Depending on the incident and the individual, it may not be easily overcome.

Its negative effects can last for many years, deeply scarring the person, and ultimately hindering their relationship with the Lord. Compared to others' experiences, mine was minimal. However at that time, and with my state of mind, it could have been my undoing.

I explained in an earlier chapter, how I was first introduced to the church Bae attended. Moving from Cali, it was to be my new church home too. I liked it. The Word went forth with power. Remember the choir and the Pastor, (who sang like Marvin)? I thought I would fit in well there, and was looking forward to perhaps serving again in the music ministry. When I returned from visiting Bae in Florida that first time, I was comforted because I felt *we* had found a church home comparable to the ones we were leaving in Cali. Its smaller size made the Pastor more accessible, and Bae even seemed to have developed a rapport with him. That did my heart good because I wanted Bae's faith to flourish while in transition, even without me.

A year later though, things were *very* different! Bae and the Pastor were now "*buddies*"—the kind that hung out occasionally, joked around, and whispered secrets. I discovered that the same woman who rummaged through my things in the condo, also attended the church. In fact, her and Bae's relationship was widely known within the church when I first visited. (No wonder the ladies were all checking me out.) I was the only one in the dark! Things were already uncomfortable at home, now they were uncomfortable at church.

It was a fact, that aside from the many people in the church who knew what was going on, the Pastor and First Lady knew too! But I didn't know they knew. So trying to maintain some dignity and hope, I scheduled a meeting with the Pastor to discuss what was happening.

It was odd, talking to a Pastor, who I knew was a friend with the very person I was complaining about. I had no idea how it would play out, so I was fidgety and guarded. I wasn't exactly sure if I was in a safe place or if our conversation would actually remain confidential—them being "boys" and all.

I think in an attempt to allay my fears, the Pastor shared, what I feel was, too much personal information about himself with me. (The First Lady of the church was not there.) I was thinking, *something is not right here.*

Surprised at some of the things he said, I was not a little comforted, and wanted to walk out. Things only worsened from there. I can't definitively say why not, but Bae and I were never counseled together. He, therefore we, simply stopped going to church. (Hmm, I wonder if he knew I met with the Pastor?) Anyway, with everything deteriorating so rapidly, I needed help. I wasn't sure where to get it at the church, knowing my personal business was so exposed, but I had nowhere else to go. Desperation caused me to seek counseling there anyway—*maybe someone there is honorable.*

The pamphlet said services were free, but I was told I had to *pay* (not offer) for any visit. I remember thinking, *What kind of church is this? Are they licensed psychiatrists? Do I need to pay for "counseling"? And if I'm suicidal? Or an unbeliever? Would they let me die and go to hell because I couldn't pay?"* I was outraged!

Cursing thoughts filled every ounce of space in my mind. I thought, *"I gave up everything to be with a man that doesn't love me! I can't get any help from this **church** unless I* pay for it! And Bae and the Pastor (of all people), are *"home-boys! I don't know what to do.* All I could do was cry. I missed my old church, my Pastor, and Cali.

Completely deterred, I forwent the whole counseling idea and tried to go it alone, but it was too heavy for me. I was very fragile, and still had nowhere to go. Three Sundays later, I managed to find my way to the church alone, but was ostracized all the more. On the surface, people were cordial, but I overheard plenty of whispering and gossiping. It was surreal—being among so many "church folk," yet so alone. *(It was no different than the job those many years ago…)*

At that time, there were two services per Sunday. I recall that particular Sunday, I decided to stay for both. I was completely broken and didn't want to leave because I had no *safe* place to go. In between services, I stayed in the pew, crying my eyes out—heavy, deep, uncontrollable sobbing for about an hour. As the expression goes, "I was toe up from the flo' up!" Still, not *one* person approached me (from the ministry to the congregation). *No one* came to see about me! *No one* came to pray with me! *No one* even touched me or said a word to me! I was distraught, devastated, destitute, and desperate, yet I was completely *ignored* in the very House of God! Hope of any help vanished. I walked out early in the second service, feeling worse than when I came in. Driving back, I thought, *"so this is what church hurt feels like?"*

Note: I cannot adequately express the gamut of my emotions then. I was so lost. There was too much happening to me in a short period of time. My mind had no time to fully process one thing before getting smashed with something else. Looking back, that experience taught me a valuable *life* lesson. Until that time, I had always been surrounded by other believers at church, work, or at home with Christian television. The blessing that comes from assembling yourself with other saints is often overlooked. There's an undergirding of strength and encouragement when you're with other people of faith. That assembly can bring hope, understanding, and revelation. I didn't have any of that then. I was on my own. I have learned the importance of being rooted and grounded in the Word of God. When there's nobody with you, nobody for you, and nobody beside you, you have to be like David and encourage yourself!

Summarizing the story in 1 Samuel 30:1-8, an enemy came and raided David's camp, while he and his men were away in battle. Upon their return, they found their camp burned, and their wives and children taken captive. Grieving, the men blamed David and spoke of stoning him, although he faced the same heartbreak they did. Being a man after God's own heart, David encouraged himself and found strength in the Lord, who counseled him and guided his steps. God told David to pursue, and that he would recover all without fail.

There may be a time when you're hit hard and you're alone. You won't be able to turn to the right or to the left for help, and you have no ally to call. It is then that you must dig deep to find your *own* strength in the Lord. It's hard, but it can be done. I had Word in me but my focus was on the wrong things. My affections had been on worldly things, and those things distracted me, and weakened me. This is why the Word of God must be your foundation! You *must* spend time with the Lord, and in the Word.

Faith comes by hearing, and hearing by the Word of God. You must read, meditate, and study. The Holy Spirit is your Helper, your Comforter, and your Strength. With Him, "Out of your belly shall flow rivers of *living* water" (John 7:38, emphasis added).

Liken this unto the parable in Luke 6:47-49 about the wise and foolish builders. The wise builder digs deep and lays a foundation before building upon it so that his structure is solid and can withstand any storm. The foolish builder is impatient and shortsighted. It's just a matter of time before collapse, because he's ill prepared for calamitous times.

I had been under solid teaching so I had a foundation, but I was crushed in my emotions and my spirit broken. God was still there to help. He stayed with me during that crucial season. He was already covering me and protecting me, but I was oblivious. Every now and then, I'd have a *moment* of clarity. I believe the Holy Spirit stirred up the Word within me, to sustain me. I may not have received it in the natural, but Spirit to spirit, I believe it strengthened my soul and helped me to keep going.

Now on a very different note, the word "Christian" is used rather loosely in our society today. Often, the title is based on family tradition, popularity, or a fragmented knowledge of religion, but many lack the understanding of having a relationship with Christ. The word itself means Christ follower. It does not mean that the person has perfected life on this Earth! True Christ followers strive to be more like Him in character, but it is a lifelong process. **At times, it takes great effort and sacrifice to achieve change in just a small area.**

Growing and maturing in Christ is a personal commitment that one has to *choose daily*. But this change requires time. It requires time to let go of traditions and people; time to release vices and prejudices; time to transform your thinking and change from your old way of doing things; time to recognize the Voice of the Holy Spirit *and* to listen to Him.

Change occurs from the inside out, but it is not immediate. It's dependent upon the amount of time you put into your relationship with Jesus. Spending quality time with Him, will show you who *you* are, and remove your focus from finding fault with others. So while that church hurt is inexcusable, *it was not the Lord that hurt you.* It was the enemy, manipulating others' weaknesses and shortcomings, in an effort to keep you from a closer relationship with God.

See, the enemy is after your soul too, and you don't have all the time in the world to figure that out. Regardless of what was said or done at the church, you still need a personal relationship with the Lord for yourself. I know it's not easy, but you must forgive that person(s) and let it go. It doesn't mean they were right or justified with what they did. And by no means are you weak or insignificant if you let it go. It's actually the opposite—*you* are the stronger one! Matthew 6:14-15 says, "For *if* you forgive men their trespasses, your heavenly Father *will* also forgive you.

> *See, the enemy is after your soul too, and you don't have all the time in the world to figure that out.*

But if you do not forgive men their trespasses, *neither will your heavenly Father forgive your trespasses."* (NKJV emphasis added)

God never promised life would be easy. He promised He would never leave you nor forsake you. Turn everything over to God and let Him fight the battle for you —He has a perfect record! Matthew 12:36-37 (NKJV) states, "But I say to you that for every idle word men may speak, they will give account of it on the day of judgment. For by your words you will be justified, and by your words you will be condemned." Keep in mind, each one of us will be accountable for the good and bad we've said and done too. We will have our *personal* one-on-one "meeting" with the Lord for judgment (Roman's 14:10b, 12). Will you be accused then, of the very things you accuse others of? Will you want the same justice you're seeking for them or would you desire Mercy? Think about that.

I'm not suggesting you act like a "doormat" for people to walk on. I'm asking you to fight your way through the circumstance with your eyes on Jesus. Sisters and Brothers, we are a flawed people and always will be. In this life, we will be hurt over and over again, but it is God's will that we learn grace and forgiveness towards others, the same way we received it from Him. Return to God, the Lover of your soul. Let *Him* strengthen you and heal you. Don't allow the actions or inactions of others to prevent you from receiving the greatest opportunity ever given to mankind—the precious Gift of having a love relationship with Jesus Christ the Savior; the One who suffered for *all* your sins on the Cross, so that you may live. Amen.

CHAPTER 19

NUGGETS & PEARLS
Gleaning Wisdom

I f you are a child of God, He uses every negative thing you go through in life to benefit you. You learn the lesson from it, He'll give you the blessing from it. It's one thing to know something with head knowledge, but it's an entirely different thing to know that same knowledge with the *heart*. When you know something in your heart (spirit), it's usually rooted there and cannot be easily shaken or removed. It produces wisdom and guidance. It's what happened to me after that season. I had a better understanding of God's way of doing things, and trusted Him more. I learned how to pray and seek His face in *all* things. To guard my eye-gates, my ear-gates, and my thoughts. To talk back to the devil and declare God's Word in the atmosphere. To cast down imaginations and suit up in the full armor of God.

God reaffirmed His deep love for me. That He is *always* for me. That the love of Christ passes all knowledge, and the peace of Christ, all understanding. Even with that, it took a long time to get out from under that burden because it was an extremely heavy weight for me then.

I heard Pastor T. D. Jakes once say that injury and recovery both have pain—their pain just has different purposes. Oh how very true that is! The road to my downfall was subtle and quick. My road to recovery was laborious and exhausting. Both processes were methodical and agonizing with conflicting purposes. One was meant to destroy me, the other, to restore me. Had God not covered me, the culmination of my sins plus the consequences from them, would have been too much for me. They would have triumphed over me, and altered the very course of my life. But bless the mighty name of Jesus, defeat was not my portion! If God be for me, *who* can be against me? I am grateful every day for my life here! "*Here*", among the living! "*Here*", in my right mind! And "*here*", living free, instead of locked up somewhere. I know I owe Him *everything*, therefore I say, "Because thy lovingkindness is better than life, my lips shall *forever* praise thee" (Psalm 63:3 emphasis added).

This is my "takeaways" chapter. These are pearls of wisdom, and little nuggets that I tucked away in my heart from that season. Each of them resonated deeply in my soul, and played an integral part in my healing and growth. They are all very personal to me but I'm sharing them with you, hoping you'll find some value in them.

Remember, one perfectly strategized setup from the enemy, could set you back years or wipe you out. That's his job—he comes to steal, kill, and destroy. I've lived that. So always be vigilant and alert, because the enemy is cunning and subtle. Be the watchman on the wall. God knows our whole life's story, when we can't see the next few seconds. Therefore, our ability to choose is a precious and powerful *gift*. Cherish it, and *choose* to trust the Lord, at *all* times! Wait on Him. I can promise you that He *is* interested, and cares about every aspect of your life—down to the most trivial detail. So ask, seek, knock. Invite Him in. Include Him in all things. Remind Him of His Word. His promises. Nothing concerning you, escapes Him. The end result is a multitude of blessings that you are not prepared for!

❖This first mention was new territory for me at the time, but wow, was it eye-opening! Obviously, I learned this the hard way, being void of understanding, so my interpretation comes solely from my experience and what I feel God later revealed to me.

I think I can safely say that nine times out of ten, if you are on any assignment from the Lord, it involves at least one other person. Whatever it is you are to do, means you already possess the necessary tools/talent to help meet that individual's need(s). With that in mind, my word to you is this: MAKE SURE YOU DO NOT GET "*INVOLVED*" WITH THE ASSIGNMENT!

> *MAKE SURE YOU DO NOT GET "INVOLVED" WITH THE ASSIGNMENT!*

That may seem obvious, maybe even ridiculous to some, but I had *no* knowledge about any of this! I still believe I did the right thing back then, reaching out to that late night DJ when he was in distress. My heart was burdened, and I felt God's compassion for him. He was saved and serving God, but life's circumstances had beaten him down, making him an easy target on the enemy's radar. Once I jumped in, I became a target too. It became a twofer for the enemy—something I did not understand at the time. You should know the enemy has studied, and continues to study, *you* as well. Don't think because he's not on your radar that you're not on his! I warned you that he's subtle and crafty. I was still healing then, and didn't know how vulnerable I was. I described how easy and comfortable Bae's and my friendship was early on. I got "too familiar" with Bae, (not part of the assignment), and lost my hedge of protection. I didn't realize I had long since wandered outside my covering from the Lord. The enemy was in! And thus my fall began.

Therefore, when you are on assignment, you *must* stay vigilant! Get closer to the Lord so your ear is always attentive. Being closer to Him has two major benefits. First, it *releases* revelation and direction *within* the assignment. Second, it *exposes* the enemy's traps to ensnare you. Stay on course, finish the assignment, then wait for God to release you from it. Any "*extra*" blessing won't be revealed until it is completed. If you veer off course in the middle, you disrupt God's plan for both your lives, and open the door for a *legal* onslaught from the enemy.

WARNING: The barrage of consequences through that open door, will surely be a tremendously heavy burden to bear, especially because it was *never* intended for your life! *You* deviated! Still, God is good. He will love you even through that process to get you back on track, the same way He did me. I'm so grateful that in His infinite Grace and Mercy, He never gives us what we truly deserve. His heart is always tender toward us.

❖ I'm going to briefly discuss this next one in case you've never heard of it before: God's Perfect Will and God's Permissive Will.

God's perfect will is *His divine will* for our lives. His permissive will is what *He allows to take place* in our lives. With both perfect and permissive will, God is always in control. His hand is on His children, whether in or out of His divine will, rightly knowing the beginning and the end. Both wills come with trials and struggles, but there is a difference between the two. The difference is, with God's perfect will, you are "covered," so to speak. There is an impenetrable force field surrounding you. *He* orders your steps, and delivers wise counsel. Even through a difficult trial, He's there strengthening you and propelling you towards greatness, *because* you have surrendered control and trust to Him. There is no safer place to be than in the perfect will of God.

Contrarily, by stubbornness, disobedience, or when you think you know better than God does, you end up in His permissive will. Most certainly, the Holy Spirit tried to turn you in a different direction before. Maybe He tried to discourage or block you from a particular person, place, or thing, but you didn't listen. So God allowed it. God knew this route would bring unnecessary hardships, but you wanted what *you* wanted. Many of those trials/struggles were never meant for you. But because you thought your way was right, you traveled a road never intended for you.

An example of this would be in the Book of Exodus where God had a perfect plan for His chosen people once He freed them from bondage from the Egyptians. They *saw* His great miracles, signs, and wonders at every step. Yet they forgot—constantly murmuring and complaining in their own selfishness. Because of that, He allowed them to have what they whined about (permissive will) but it cost them their very lives! Their "rebellious" hearts caused them to wander in the wilderness for forty years, on an eleven day trip, instead of receiving the Goodness of God's Promise. Out of more than 600,000 people, only two from that generation remained alive to actually enter into the Promised Land.

So yes, with your way you could *possibly* reach your destination, but at what cost to you? Don't be fooled, outside of God's will, there *will* be a price to pay!

On the other hand, you may *never* reach your destination, or the one God had for you! Your season of opportunity could pass while you are wandering around in the wilderness, and some opportunities do not come around a second time. So why settle for almost when you can have the utmost?

Take heart, God is so awesome! If you repent and cry out to Him, He hears you. He comes to the rescue and redirects you to another path of His choosing, so that you still arrive at His desired destination for you. His word says, "For I know the thoughts that I think toward you, says the Lord, thoughts of peace and not of evil, to give you a future and a hope" (Jeremiah 29:11 NKJV).

On this note, was it your decision that caused your derailment, with all its consequences?

Your rebelliousness? Disobedience? His promise doesn't change; He'll stay with you. I tell you, it's much better to trust God first or realign yourself with His will. Choose to help yourself succeed, avoiding the costly snares and pitfalls from the enemy. Stay close to Him, pray, and follow His direction. In Him is life, and that more abundantly (John 10:10).

❖Now if you've never heard the expression, *"sugar on the floor"* before, let me ask you this question: What good is sugar on the floor?

It's no good; it's useless. It's swept up with the other dirt and discarded as trash. Its purpose is nullified, and its destiny, never fulfilled. I told you how much I loved Bae. I was good to him, and my love for him was genuine and whole. God even rebuked me for it! I really believed we would have been an influential and powerful couple for the Body. But it turned out, *I was just sugar on the floor.* From that, I struggled with worthlessness, inferiority, and inadequacy for a long time; I had given him all of me. I almost lost everything, but through the Grace of God, I didn't.

In my healing process, I came across a quote from the late Maya Angelou that resonated in my soul and spirit. To this day, it's one of my mantras. It says: "A woman's heart should be so hidden in God that a man has to seek Him to find her." (Ladies, read that one more time!) Woman of God, I pray this revelation takes root in your spirit as you meditate on it. *Really think about it.* You are *never* to be sugar on the floor! You're made in the image of God. You *are His,* and you are far more valuable than you realize! *He* is the lover of your soul, *and He truly loves you*—totally and completely; unconditionally and eternally!

Ladies, I believe you want a relationship that is going to last. So don't entangle yourself in a bunch of soul ties (Galatians 5:1), or with people that don't or won't appreciate you. Walk in a way that is pleasing to the Lord. While you're waiting, (not looking), prepare yourself to be a faithful helpmeet. Your position as a wife is a very crucial role for your Man of God. I've learned it's not just a title, it's an office. The Bible says in Proverbs 18:22 (NKJV), that he who finds a wife finds a good thing, and obtains favor from the Lord. So let that man find you hidden in God, your Protector. In the meantime, prepare *yourself*. Pray. And wait. God will do the vetting.

❖ One of my favorite scriptures is Psalm 103:1-5 (NKJV). I memorized this in my earlier years, and usually personalize it when I pray. It reads: Bless the Lord, O my soul, And all that is within me, bless His holy name! (vs.2) Bless the Lord, O my soul, and forget not all His benefits. (vs.3) Who forgives all your (*my*) iniquities, Who heals all your (*my*) diseases, (vs.4) Who redeems your (*my*) life from destruction, Who crowns you (*me*) with lovingkindness and tender mercies, (vs.5) Who satisfies your (*my*) mouth with good things, So that your (*my*) youth is renewed like the eagle's.

This one scripture sums up so much of God's Goodness in those five verses! Really take a look at what God does. HE forgives! HE heals! HE redeems (saves)! HE crowns (blesses)! HE satisfies (provides)! And HE renews! Glory to God! This is so powerful! I know at times we need to hear something over and over before it really sinks in. I made it a point to remind myself every day of these magnificent Blessings towards me, in spite of all the things I had done.

Memorize a few scriptures that resonate with your soul. Keep them in your arsenal for recall. Use them to encourage yourself, to fortify your faith, or simply remind you of God's Goodness. Look up to where your Help comes from (Psalm 121), *always* keeping a praise on your lips and gratitude in your heart.

❖ The "F" word: FORGIVENESS

It may seem like a *"dirty"* word considering what some of you may have been through, but I can assure you, it is a gold nugget for your treasure box. Matthew 6:14-15 (NKJV) tells us, "For if we forgive men their trespasses, your heavenly Father will also forgive you: But if you do not forgive men their trespasses, neither will your Father forgive your trespasses."

There is no arguing with the Word! There are no exceptions or "what if" scenarios. It says what it means and it means what it says. What I have learned is, *unforgiveness only hurts you*! I know it may not seem that way, but the damage it causes you is far worse than the damage caused to the other person. Most of the time, you get stuck holding on to the pain, while the other person has moved on with his/her life. They don't know, or care what's happening with you. I know that's a hard truth to hear.

What you experienced was devastating, and letting someone "off the hook" seems unreasonable and unfair. It's natural to want revenge. **But let me share this secret: the best revenge is to forgive and release that person(s) to the Lord.** Remember God prompting me to email Bae? By releasing them, you decide to let the Lord deal with them and handle the situation for you. I understand you probably don't want to hear that, (I didn't), and the last thing on your mind is anything "Godly." We've already discussed some of the benefits before, (Chapter 18), but the truth is, forgiveness is a *command* from God, not a request.

Think of the kind of person you were when God forgave you? Matthew 10:8b reminds us that we have freely received; we should freely give. Even with this, you have free will whether or not to obey, though it is in your best interest to do so. It's a choice, but it must be a *true* act of the *heart* and not the mouth. Of course it's not easy—but it *is absolutely necessary!* This decision benefits both you and the other person(s). You, because there will no longer be an open door giving the enemy access, hindering your prayers, or blocking your blessings. You will no longer be trapped under the yoke of bondage through *your own sin* of unforgiveness, and God can begin His healing process in you. Your countenance, attitude, and overall health will improve. Your peace and joy will return. And you will think and see things differently.

If you continue to take matters into your own hands, God won't interfere. But if you decide to trust Him, He will take control. Only The Creator knows how to deal with every one of us individually. Like it or not, God loves that person too. His desire is for that "offender" to also grow and mature in the ways of the Lord. If they don't know Him, He desires that they come to know Him through salvation (2 Peter 3:9).

God will work it out, but His timing is not our timing, nor His methods like ours (Isaiah 55:8-9). We don't have to "like" it or understand it; we simply have to trust

Him. Once you release that person to the Lord, He can begin to work in them as well.

Note: God's unique perspective and way of doing things have the ability to benefit and bless *all* involved, because He gives Grace and Mercy to them, just like He does you. But He is still a just God. The Bible says, (Matthew 5:45b), "*...for He makes His sun rise on the evil and the good, and sends rain on the just and the unjust."* This simply means that everyone is afforded the same opportunities; that God is no respecter of persons. Your willingness to listen and obey however, will determine the kind of fruit you yield on the road you travel. Forgiveness is an essential key.

I once read about the Japanese art of Kintsugi. The word itself means "to join with gold." It is the unique art of repairing broken glass or ceramic pottery with gold lacquer. The philosophy behind it is to fix something rather than discard it, believing the final product is more beautiful and valuable than it was at first.

In the Bible, gold is symbolic of many things. It's associated in different passages with wealth, power, royalty, and God's Glory.

Let's apply this philosophy biblically to God and His way of doing things. He sees and knows every detail about each of us. He has promised that if we trust Him, He will take all the "broken" things in our lives, and use them to prosper us according to His purpose. (Romans 8:28 AMP) This means *none* of your suffering, in any area, is wasted. What a promise! Everything secret will be revealed and anything hidden will come to light. God knows everything. It's *your* attitude that will determine your outcome. Therefore, pray. Keep your heart clean. Practice the Fruit of the Spirit (Galatians 5:22-23). Honor Him with your dependence, obedience, and gratitude. *In* everything, (not *for* everything), give thanks: for this is the will of God in Christ Jesus concerning you (1 Thessalonians 5:18).

If you're willing to wait on God, nothing will take very long. Before you realize it, you will see the unveiling of the *Master's* magnificent *kintsugi,* collected and created from the broken pieces of your life.

 Your willingness to listen and obey however, will determine the kind of fruit you yield on the road you travel.

CHAPTER 20

HE IS... YOU ARE
Embracing Identity

As I thought about all this, it served as a reminder then, and now, that there were so many ways and so many days where my life could have taken a turn for the worse—but God! *Everyday*, we should be grateful and give Him thanks for protecting us from things seen and unseen, known and unknown. I am so grateful to be alive! I'm grateful to be in my right mind! Grateful to be healthy! Grateful to be free! And extraordinarily grateful to be loved by God! So in this chapter, I want to remind you of Who God is, and who we are in Him.

HE IS…Elohim; ²Jehovah; ³God Almighty! HE'S The ⁴Great I Am and ⁵The Ancient of Days! HE'S ⁶Alpha and Omega—The First and The Last; The Beginning and the End! HE'S ⁷Yahweh, ⁸The One who is, and was, and is to come! HE'S ⁹Omniscient, Omnipotent, Ubiquitous, ¹⁰Magnificent, and ¹¹Majestic! HE'S ¹²Emmanuel—God with us! HE'S ¹³Master and ¹⁴Ruler; ¹⁵Savior and ¹⁶Redeemer, The ¹⁷Creator of Heaven and Earth! HE'S ¹⁸King of kings and Lord of lords! HE'S ¹⁹The Light of the world—²⁰The Bright and Morning Star! HE'S ²¹The Rose of Sharon, The ²²Balm of Gilead, and ²³The Lily of the Valley! HE'S ²⁴The Bread of Life, ²⁵The Lion from the tribe of Judah, ²⁶The Lamb of God, and The ²⁷Prince of Peace! HE IS ²⁸The Way, The Truth, and The Life! HE'S ²⁹Yeshua and the ³⁰Author and Finisher of our faith! HE'S ³¹The Good Shepherd, our ³²Helper, our ³³Comforter, our ³⁴Counselor, and our ³⁵Banner! HE'S our ³⁶Refuge, our ³⁷Fortress, our ³⁸Shield, and our ³⁹Buckler! HE IS our ⁴⁰Strong Tower, ⁴¹The Rock on which we stand! HE'S The ⁴²Burden Remover and The ⁴³Yoke Destroyer, The ⁴⁴Breach Repairer, and ⁴⁵The Lifter of our heads! HE'S The ⁴⁶Deliverer, ⁴⁷Provider, ⁴⁸Healer, and ⁴⁹Protector! HE'S The ⁵⁰Mind Regulator, The ⁵¹Heart Fixer, The ⁵²Way Maker, and The ⁵³Promise Keeper! HE'S our ⁵⁴Joy, our ⁵⁵Peace, our ⁵⁶Strength, and our ⁵⁷Breath! HE'S The ⁵⁸Friend that sticks closer than a brother and our ⁵⁹Faithful Witness! HE'S The ⁶⁰Lamp unto our feet and The Light unto our paths! HE'S ⁶¹Perfect — ⁶²Holy, ⁶³Righteous, ⁶⁴Just, ⁶⁵Loving, Longsuffering and Merciful! ⁶⁶HE is the same, yesterday, today, and forever! HE'S ⁶⁷The Lord of Hosts and ⁶⁸The King of Glory! HE'S ⁶⁹The Messiah— ⁷⁰The Only

Begotten Son of The Father! **HE IS** [71]**JESUS,** [72]**THE CHRIST!** And [73]HE overcame the world, death, hell, and the grave! [74]**HE IS RISEN**, and is [75]seated at the right hand of God, forevermore! [76]For Thine is the kingdom, and the power, and the glory forever. Amen.

(In Him)**YOU ARE...**[1]fearfully and wonderfully made, (not an accident or an afterthought)! You are [2]*His* creation, made in the image and likeness of God, [3]perfectly designed by The Master Potter! You were [4]bought at a price you can never repay! You are [5]saved, [6]delivered, and [7]set free from bondage! [8]You are a new creature in Christ—the *old* things have passed away! [9]You are washed clean by The Blood of The Lamb; [10]your body is the Temple of The Holy Ghost! You are [11]forgiven, and [12]reconciled unto The Father - [13]redeemed, [14]renewed, [15]sealed! [16]You are a child of The King, [17]Abraham's seed, and an heir according to The Promise! [18]You are a chosen generation, a royal priesthood, an holy nation, and a peculiar people! [19]You are blessed and highly favored by God! [20]You are blessed in the city and blessed in the field, blessed going out and blessed coming in! [21]You are the head and not the tail, above and not beneath! [22]You are a lender not a borrower; a leader and not a follower! You are a [23]lively stone, the [24]salt of the Earth, and the light of the world! You are [25]justified, [26]appointed, and [27]anointed, [28]holy, [29]righteous, and [30]sanctified! [31]You are healed, whole, and prosperous! [32]You are a conqueror and an [33]overcomer, with [34]power and authority in Jesus' name! [35]You are a servant of The Master and a good steward! [36]You are the apple of God's eye; [37]a crown of glory, and a royal diadem!

You are deeply desired and unconditionally loved by Him—with an inexplicable, unparalleled, immeasurable, and unfathomable Love! Hallelujah and Bless His Holy Name!

 There is no greater Love!

THE AWAKENING
Becoming the Warrior

I never did get any closure from Bae. In fact, I never saw him again. Consequently, I allowed my life to be stagnant for years because of it, while God was trying to pull me out. You must move from that place to survive! God will give you the closure you need.

It was in this place that I learned to fight in the spirit. It was neither quick nor easy. I had to learn to fight with faith in the Word and not my emotions. I had to put on my armor daily and stand my ground, although every day it looked like nothing was changing.

You too, must learn to fight for yourself! Refuse to stay entangled in bondage with that heavy yoke around your neck. Trade in the mask you're hiding behind, (with its limited and false protection), for the full armor of God, which covers you from your head to your feet! Yes, it can be exhausting, but *you are in a fight!* God has given you the tools you need, to not only fight, but to win! You have the written Word, which is your sword. You have pastors, teachers, sermons, sisters and brothers who have already prevailed, and are living testimonies. And most of all you have the Lord on your side, guiding you, and giving you power to overcome! *He has already declared you victorious!* You will win, but you have to do your part.

It will be God alone that gets the glory for your victory, so I don't have a perfect step-by-step plan to give you. I can only offer you a guideline. Everyone's process is different, and God will give you strategic instructions relating to your personal situation. I know you *must* trust Him. Based on experience I will add that if you can pray in your heavenly prayer language, do it—often. This will bring answers the enemy is not privy to. If you don't have your prayer language yet, learn to pray spirit to Spirit, from the deepest recesses of your heart to God's—the same way Hannah poured her heart out before the Lord (1 Samuel 1:1-16 NKJV). God does hear the thoughts and intents of the heart, the devil cannot.

Either way, you are to P.U.S.H. – **P**ray **U**ntil **S**omething **H**appens. Prayer does change things! And faith causes walls to fall and mountains to move. Together, they are an unstoppable force that gets God's attention, and summons help from Heaven. God and you are the majority! Consult the Lord in every area. Trust His guidance wholeheartedly. Listen to the Voice of the Holy Spirit, and be obedient. The name of Jesus has power, healing, and life in it! *In His name, you will win!*

Beloved, I've done my best to share what I feel the Lord told me to. I pray my testimony has encouraged you or shed some light in a dark area.

No matter where you are right now, I can assure you, God has much more for you—more than you can ask, think, or imagine.

Know that you are *not* defined by what others have said or say about you. You are *not* defined by your mistakes, failures, or circumstances. The *true* definition of who you are, comes from how *God* sees you, and who *He* says you are! That is the only validation you need! *He is* your *key* to *life and success! He* has the abundance of goodness and blessings that await you. So throw off the cloaks of bitterness, rejection, depression, (and all their relatives), and dare to walk in your desired freedom with the Lord. Let the Word of God wash you, deliver you, heal you, and cover you. *For where the Spirit of the Lord is, there is freedom, and if the Son sets you free, you are free indeed* (2 Corinthians 3:17; John 8:36 NIV).

 God will give you the closure you need.

THE FULL ARMOR OF GOD

¹⁰ Finally, my brethren, be strong in the Lord, and in the power of his might.

¹¹ Put on the whole armour of God, that ye may be able to stand against the wiles of the devil.

¹² For we wrestle not against flesh and blood, but against principalities, against powers, against the rulers of the darkness of this world, against spiritual wickedness in high places.

¹³ Wherefore take unto you the whole armour of God, that ye may be able to withstand in the evil day, and having done all, to stand.

¹⁴ Stand therefore, having your loins girt about with truth, and having on the breastplate of righteousness;

¹⁵ And your feet shod with the preparation of the gospel of peace;

¹⁶ Above all, taking the shield of faith, wherewith ye shall be able to quench all the fiery darts of the wicked.

¹⁷ And take the helmet of salvation, and the sword of the Spirit, which is the word of God:

¹⁸ Praying always with all prayer and supplication in the Spirit, and watching thereunto with all perseverance and supplication for all saints;

Ephesians 6:10-18

"AWAKENING" PRAYER

Father God, in the name of Jesus, I come to you broken and in distress. I realize I can't make it without You. I repent of all my wrongdoing and cry out to You now for help. I lay everything that's not like You, down at Your feet.

I cast aside the old things that had me bound, and not living the life You died to give me. I reject the spirits of pain, bitterness, resentment, hatred, and anger. I stand against the spirits of unforgiveness, abandonment, isolation, rejection, and mind control. I rebuke and cast out the spirits of shame, insecurity, inadequacy, inferiority, and low self esteem; and I bind those spirits of depression, despair, anxiety, suicide, and homicide. I declare that no weapon formed against me shall prosper, and I command every spirit not of God, to release its hold on me, in the name of Jesus!

I announce I am a child of the Most High God! I am precious in His sight and I embrace His Goodness! I plead the Blood of Jesus over me and declare I have the mind of Christ! I declare I am free and break all bonds of the enemy. I loose healing, health, wellness, and wholeness into every area of my life. I claim the abundant life God has for me from this moment forward, and I walk in His Divine favor! I bless You Lord, and receive this all by faith, in the powerful name of Jesus, Amen.

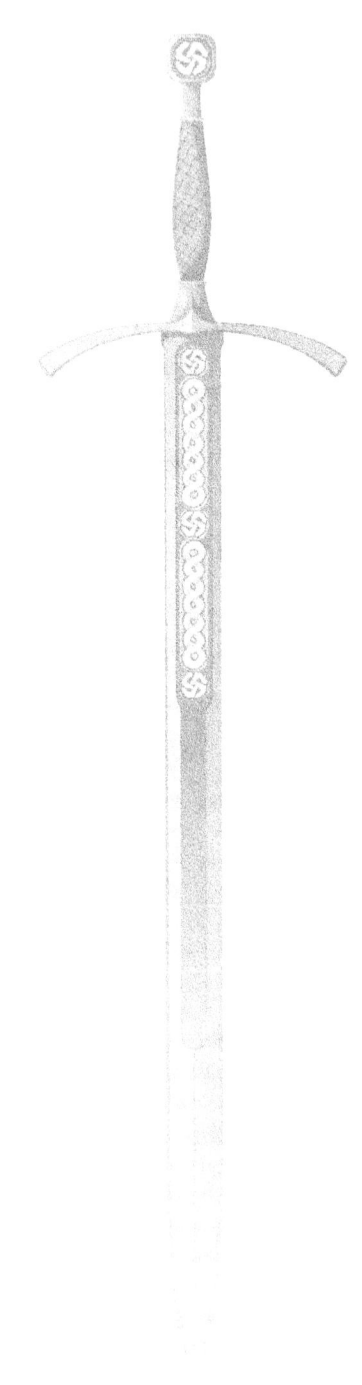

PRAYER OF SALVATION

If you've *never accepted Jesus Christ as your personal Savior, or if you need to **recommit yourself to the Lord, I invite you to say one the following prayers aloud:

*Father God, I admit that I'm a sinner in need of a Savior. I repent of my sins. I believe that Jesus came in the flesh, was crucified, died, rose from the dead, and is alive and seated at Your right hand. I confess with my mouth and believe in my heart that Jesus is Lord, and I'm now born again. In Jesus' name, amen.

**Heavenly Father, I have sinned and acknowledge that I have wandered away from You. I choose to rededicate my life and serve You with my whole heart. I repent and ask Your forgiveness for all my wrongdoing. Create in me a clean heart, O Lord, and renew a right spirit within me. In Jesus' name, I pray, amen.

If you said either of those prayers and meant it, welcome, or welcome back, to the family! If you don't own one, get a Bible that teaches the uncompromised Word of God. Then find a reputable church in your area to join, that does the same. Begin to walk with the Lord and grow in the Word, that your ways may be pleasing to Him.

I pray the Lord bless you and keep you always. May He give to you the spirit of revelation in the knowledge of Him. May the eyes of your understanding be enlightened, that you may know what is the hope of His calling, what are the riches of the glory of His inheritance in the saints, and what is the exceeding greatness of His power toward us that believe, from this time forward and evermore. Amen

SCRIPTURAL REFERENCE
PAGE 124

HE IS: [1]Genesis 1:1(AMP); [2]Psalm 83:18; [3]Exodus 6:3; [4]Exodus 3:14; [5]Daniel 7:9; [6]Revelation 22:13; [7]Exodus 3:15(TJB); [8]Revelation 1:8; [9]Psalm 139; [10]Psalm 145:3 (MSG); [11]Psalm 93:1 (AMP); [12]Matthew 1:23; [13]Jeremiah 32:17(MSG); [14]1 Chronicles 29:12(AMP); [15]Matthew 1:21; [16]Isaiah 44:24; [17]Genesis 1:1; [18]Revelation 19:16; [19]John 8:21; [20]Revelation 22:26; [21]Song of Solomon 2:1; [22]Jeremiah 8:22; [23]Song of Solomon 2:1; [24]John 6:35; [25]Revelation 5:5; [26]John 1:36; [27]Isaiah 9:6; [28]John 14:6; [29]Mark 12:1 (CJB); [30]Hebrews 12:2; [31]John 10:11; [32]Psalm 54:4(AMP); [33]2 Corinthians 1:3-4; [34]Isaiah 9:6; [35]Exodus 17:15(AMP); [36]Psalm 46:1; [37]Psalm 31:3; [38]Psalm 28:7(ESV); [39]Psalm 91:4; [40]Proverbs 18:10; [41]Proverbs 18:2; [42]Matthew 11:28; [43]Isaiah 10:27; [44]Isaiah 58:12(AMP); [45]Psalm 3:3; [46]Psalm 50:15; [47]Philippians 4:19; [48]Psalm 103:3; 2 [49]Thessalonians 3:3(NIV); [50]Isaiah 26:3(NKJV); [51]Psalm 147:3; [52]Isaiah 45:2; [53]Numbers 23:19, 2 Corinthians 1:20; [54]John 15:11; [55]Ephesians 2:14; [56]Psalm 28:7; [57]Genesis 2:7, Job 12:10; [59]Proverbs 18:24; Revelation 1:5(AMP); [60]Psalm 119:10; [61]Matthew 5:48; [62]Isaiah 6:3; [63]Psalm 145:17; [64]Deuteronomy 32:4(AMP); [65]1 John 4:8; [66]Hebrews 13:6; [67]Isaiah 6:3; [68]Psalm 24:7-10(AMP); [69]John 4:25-26; [70]John 3:16; [71]Matthew 1:21; [72]Matthew 16:16; [73]John 16:33, Revelation 1:18; [74]Matthew 28:6-7(NKJV); [75]Ephesians 1:20; [76]Matthew 6:13b.

YOU ARE: [1]Psalm 139:14; [2]Genesis 1:26-27; [3]Isaiah 64:8; [4]1Corinthians 6:20(AMP); [5]Roman's 10:19, Ephesians 2:8; [6]Psalm 107:6; [7]Galatians 5:1; [8]2 Corinthians 5:17; [9]Hebrews 9:14; [10]1Corinthians 6:19-20(AMP); [11]1John 1:9; [12]Roman's 5:10; [13]Roman's 3:24; [14]Ephesians 4:22-24; [15]Ephesians 1:13; [16]John 1:12(AMP); [17]Galatians 3:29, Roman's 8:17); [18]1Peter 2:9; [19]Psalm 1:1-3, Psalm 90:17(NIV); [20]Deuteronomy 28:3,6; [21]Deuteronomy 28:13 [22]Deuteronomy 28:2-13; [23]1 Peter 2:5; [24]Matthew 5:13-14; [25]Roman's 3:24; [26]John 15:16(AMP); [27]2 Corinthians 1:21(AMP); [28]1 Peter 1:15-16; [29]2 Corinthians 5:21(AMP); [30]1 Corinthians 6:11; [31]Isaiah 53:5; [32]Romans 8:35,37; [33]Revelation 12:11; [34]2 Timothy 1:7, Luke 10:19(AMP); [35]1 Corinthians 3:9(NRSV); [36]Psalm 17:8; [37]Isaiah 62:3.

ABOUT THE AUTHOR

Patrice E. Hughley was introduced to the Christian faith in the 1980s. Having accepted Jesus Christ as her Lord and Savior, she first learned under the late Apostle Frederick K. C. Price, of Crenshaw Christian Center, then studied under Bishop Charles E. Blake, of West Angeles Church of God in Christ.

She deeply desires to help those who feel stagnant or lost because of a broken heart to understand there is a way out of that darkness to a beautiful and healthy life again.

YOU WRITE, WE PUBLISH,
TOGETHER WE CREATE...

DIVINE WORKS PUBLISHING, LLC.

A co-publishing service for indie authors seeking a strategic bigger partner alliance for greater success in today's marketplace.

www.DivineWorksPublishing.com

561-990-BOOK (2665)

info@ DivineWorksPublishing.com

www.ingramcontent.com/pod-product-compliance
Lightning Source LLC
Chambersburg PA
CBHW070058080526
44586CB00013B/1107